salads

salads

starters, mains and sides

Elsa Petersen-Schepelern

photography by Peter Cassidy

RYLAND
PETERS
& SMALL
LONDON NEW YORK

Dedicated to Ron and Kirsten Bray

Senior Designer Susan Downing

Editor Katherine Steer

Production Patricia Harrington

Art Director Gabriella Le Grazie

Publishing Director Alison Starling

Food Stylist Linda Tubby

Prop Stylist Róisín Nield

Indexer Hilary Bird

First published in hardback in Great Britain in 2003

This paperback edition published in 2008
by Ryland Peters & Small
20–21 Jockey's Fields, London WC1R 4BW
www.rylandpeters.com

10 9 8 7 6 5 4 3 2 1

ISBN 978 1 84597 611 8

A catalogue record for this book is available from the British Library.

Printed and bound in China.

Notes

All spoon measurements are level.

All eggs are large, unless otherwise specified. Uncooked or partly cooked
eggs should not be served to the very young, the very old, those with
compromised immune systems, or to pregnant women.

Author's Acknowledgements

As usual, I would like to thank Pete Cassidy, Linda Tubby and Róisín Nield for
their beautiful work. Thanks also to nephews Peter Bray and Luc Votan, and to
Susan, Martin, Tessa, Karen and Mike, who have tasted their way through the
testing. Friends and fellow food writers have also been generous with their time
and advice – Clare Ferguson, Sonia Stevenson, Alastair Hendy, Louise Pickford,
Kimiko Barber and Linda Tubby among others. As usual, many thanks. My
grateful thanks also to my editors, Kathy Steer, Susan Stuck and Roy Butcher,
plus designer Susan Downing, who never fails to be terrific fun as well.

contents

not just greens ...

Everyone loves a salad. It's one of the world's most versatile dishes. You can serve something small, light and elegant as a starter, something substantial and satisfying as a main course or something contrasting and crunchy as a side dish.

At elegant dinner parties, the salad often follows the main course in order to clear the palate, vying for position with the cheese, which the French serve after the main course to accompany any remaining red wine. The English serve it after as well, because if it's a green salad, some people like to mix the dressing with the meat juices. The rest of us please ourselves, and our meals are surely the more delicious because of it.

It's odd to think that the word is derived from the Latin *sal* (salt). The Romans ate vegetables and leaves with a simple dressing of salt, oil or vinegar – similar to the way they do today, in dishes like *pinzimonio* (crudités with vinaigrette). That may be why we identify dishes dressed with these three items as 'salads' when they appear in other cuisines. The Japanese serve *aemono* and *sunomono*, or 'little vinegared things', in tiny, elegant bowls. The Vietnamese have a passion for huge plates of herbs, 'table salads', which are added to many dishes. A true Vietnamese salad – or one from other countries in the region – is often dressed with fish sauce (the salt element) and lime juice (the vinegar element). Often the oil element is missing, so we can congratulate ourselves on a healthy, low-fat salad if we choose one of theirs.

In this book, I've tried to give you a taste of salads from around the world, as well as information on preparing them that I must admit is hugely opinionated, but I hope useful to you, since it is certainly based on experience.

the basics

just leaves ...

choosing

Once, leaves came in one variety – iceberg. Now, there are dozens of different kinds. Choose the one best suited to the other ingredients in the salad, or in the rest of the meal, or to your own inclinations and those of your family and friends. There are four general leaf categories; sweet and soft, crisp and crunchy, bitter or spicy.

• Sweet and soft leaves include butterhead lettuce, lamb's lettuce, oakleaf and mignonettes (cut-and-come-again lettuces).

• Crisp, crunchy leaves include iceberg, romaine and its vertically challenged cousin Little Gem.

• The bitter category includes frisée, rocket, baby spinach, radicchio, escarole and chicory.

• Hot, spicy notes are provided by watercress, and nasturtium leaves and flowers, for instance.

preparation

I think one of the world's greatest inventions has been the salad spinner. Before I was given one, I used to wash the leaves in the sink, drain them in a colander, then wrap them in a tea towel, go outside and sling my arm in circles as if I were making billy tea, a famous and undrinkable Australian beverage.

Now, I put them in the spinner, put the cage in the sink, wash them thoroughly, give them a few twirls and they're perfect. That is unless they have soft leaves, when gentler treatment is needed.

I was delighted when supermarkets introduced ready-washed puffed bags full of mixed leaves. The only problem is, I suddenly thought 'What have they been washed in, and exactly what sort of air is in the bag with them if they don't wilt like normal leaves'. And in any case the bags are always full of lollo rosso, the pariah of the lettuce world.

So – I wash them anyway, like a racoon, but I do it at the very last minute and let them drain on kitchen paper.

Jennifer Patterson, she of the Two Fat Ladies, used to keep her bowl of salad leaves out on the fire escape until she was ready to serve. She said it gave them exactly the right degree of crispness. I've tried it myself, and it's fine if you live in a cold climate, and your fire escape has signed up to the Clean Air Act. However, she was absolutely right – a bit of chill will perk them up no end.

windowboxes and flowerpots

Food writers and celebrity chefs often surprise us with unusual and hard-to-buy leaves, herbs and vegetables. These are the people responsible for introducing us to interesting and delicious ingredients – ingredients that, inevitably, become accepted day-to-day foods. In some places, even olive oil wasn't widely available until about twenty years ago, and there was a time when rocket wasn't found even in specialist greengrocers, let alone an ordinary supermarket. For today's home cooks, at least in the salad leaf and herb department, it is possible to grow your own. You don't need a huge garden to do it, either. A couple of flowerpots or windowboxes are perfectly adequate for most of our needs – and the quality of freshly picked produce will be a revelation.

A windowbox with herbs like thyme, oregano, parsley, chives and rosemary will be very useful. Most of them, thankfully, rather like dry, sunny conditions. Buy the plants from a nursery – the pots you buy for picking in supermarkets are too weak and spindly to survive ordinary life in a windowbox. You can also sow rocket seeds in a flowerpot, for an on-going supply of baby leaves. In addition, interesting Japanese herbs and leaves are now sold by specialist seed suppliers. Seed and plant suppliers are now readily accessible online and via mail order. See page 126 for contact details.

salad safety

What? Salads a safety hazard? Who would have believed it? Salad stuffs are just as prone to mishaps as any other food, especially because some of them are cooked, then cooled, then served – and this can be a trap.

Leaves and other vegetables grow in or near the ground. And soil, let's face it, is dirt. You don't know where it's been. So just wash it off thoroughly, then rinse and dry before using. That looks after dirt. What about pesticides and other baddies inflicted on the vegetable world by humans? My solution is to go for organically grown and pesticide-free produce. I prefer to buy eggs, meat and poultry that has been raised kindly and free range.

There are some foods especially prone to spoiling after cooking. Chicken, for instance, should be cooked thoroughly and, in my view, served in a salad as soon as it's cool enough to handle. Even meats that can be served rare, like beef and duck, are better warm or just cool (page 17). Interestingly, smoked items, which were originally smoked to preserve them, don't last as long because the producers know they will be kept in the refrigerator.

The surprise culprit, however, is rice. Many of us would never think of rice as dangerous, but cooked rice spoils very quickly. However, one of the best tricks I know is to stir sushi vinegar dressing through it – this will keep it fresh for up to a day (page 125).

oils, vinegars and juices

about oils

I can be infinitely pedantic about oils – you have been warned.

• Oils are better for you if they are extracted without the use of heat.

• Oils are fats – and some fats are better for you than others. Cold-pressed olive, avocado, sunflower, safflower and peanut oils are good, but corn oil and vegetable oil less so.

• Fats are not necessarily bad for you – they are necessary for hormones of all kinds, for brain function and for the proper development of babies.

• When heated, fats change to become more dangerous – all except butter. So – amazing though it may seem, butter is actually an excellent cooking medium. And it tastes wonderful. I use butter or ghee (clarified butter), but never margarine.

salad oils

• For regular salads, cold-pressed extra virgin olive oil is the best. But it has an assertive flavour. That flavour is an advantage for most foods – but for a less pronounced taste, choose a blander oil, such as peanut, sunflower or safflower. Cold pressed of course.

• For Asian salads, you will find oil is very often omitted in favour of other flavours, such as citrus juices, rice vinegars, wines and spirits, salt and its derivatives, such as soy sauce or fish sauce, or other fruit juices, such as tamarind or plum.

• Sesame oil, toasted or not, should be used as a seasoning note – not as a major ingredient. Use just a few drops with other oils. I love it with watercress.

• My other favourite seed oil is pumpkin seed, but it becomes rancid very quickly. The bottles I buy are quite large, so I decant them into smaller bottles, cork firmly and keep in a cool dark place.

nut oils

• My favourites are walnut oil, hazelnut oil and macadamia oil, but used in a ratio of about 3 parts olive oil to 1 part nut oil, otherwise they're too assertive.

• Nut oils, like seed oils, turn rancid hugely quickly. I try to buy in tiny bottles, for a particular recipe for the nut in question.

about vinegars

Vinegar forms a counterpoint to the smoothness of oils – and is sometimes used by itself.

• Wine vinegar – red and white – goes with most European dressings, especially those from wine-producing areas such as those bordering the Mediterranean. I prefer white wine vinegar. Red wine vinegar is stronger and discolours food. Please yourself.

• Champagne is just a more delicate form of white wine vinegar, and its appeal may have more to do with the romance of its name than its inherent properties.

• Sherry vinegar, on the other hand, is a much more complex and interesting flavour. One of my favourites.

• Cider vinegar is made from cider apples, and has a sweet and attractive flavour.

• Rice vinegars are very useful in salads – mild and often complex. Dark vinegars are not entirely suitable for salads, since they often have caramel added.

• Balsamic vinegar is, very often, a fraud. True balsamic is aged for years, and is very expensive. Inexpensive balsamic has, almost certainly, been made of ordinary vinegar with caramel added. To improve its flavour, Sydney food writer Louise Pickford reduces it by boiling it down by about two-thirds (see recipe page 21).

• I have never been a fan of fruit vinegars, such as raspberry, or herb vinegars, such as tarragon, believing that the fresh herb added will have more interest than an acidified old leaf. But if you like them, do use them.

• Black and white malt vinegar have no place in salads, though they were used in non-wine-producing areas before modern transport methods made them redundant.

about juices

• Lemon and lime juice can take the place of vinegars in salad dressings, and are widely used in South-east Asia with salt, sugar and spicy ingredients.

• Orange juice will perform the same function as wine vinegar, and is often used in Moroccan salads.

• Japanese umeboshi plum vinegar is divine in salads. Sweet but sharp, it has an elusive flavour that is suitable for salads other than Japanese. I like it in the Red Salad on page 56.

preparing protein

How many times have you been presented with the salad version of the rubber chicken? One of the reasons it's like that is that it's been refrigerated and not brought back to room temperature before serving. That's understandable, perhaps, in a large catering establishment, but when you cook at home you can prepare these ingredients in the most delicious way.

chicken

Roast, poach or steam the chicken in the usual way, let cool a little, then pull the flesh off the bones, in big pieces. I think chicken will taste better, with better texture, if pulled, not cut, into smaller pieces. It will taste better if you don't refrigerate it, so if you can make the salad as soon as it's cool enough to handle, or at room temperature, the flavour and texture will always be better. However, if you're keeping it for any length of time, health concerns will dictate that it must be refrigerated. Return the chicken to room temperature before serving.

duck

I pan-grill the breasts, skin side down, at low-medium heat until the fat has almost completely rendered out, about 20 minutes. Pour off the fat from time to time. Season the flesh side, then turn and cook the flesh side just until browned. The skin should be crisp, the fat mostly rendered and the flesh pinkly rare. I like the legs to be roasted until the skin is crispy, then skin and flesh pulled into shreds. This treatment is especially good for Asian salads.

beef

Beef for salads is best cooked rare, then carved into thick slices and served warm or cool. Again, refrigerators solidify the fat in meat or poultry and make it less palatable.

chickpeas, and dried peas, beans and lentils

These ingredients are just made for the salad treatment. I defy anyone not to have opened a convenient can, then rinsed, drained and dressed the contents. However, the canned versions often contain both sugar and salt, and are also more expensive than the dried versions. It would be great to be able to give you a schedule for how long each kind should be soaked, then a schedule for how long they should be boiled, but it really depends how old they were to start with, and how long they'd been kept. Keeping them for a long time doesn't mean they're not as good – it just takes longer to cook them. There are several golden rules:

• Don't presoak lentils. No need – they cook in a very short time anyway.

• To soak peas and beans, put them in a bowl, cover with cold water and soak for 8 hours or overnight. To save time, cover with boiling water and let soak for about 2 hours before cooking.

• Never add salt until the end of cooking, or about 5 minutes from the end. If you do, they'll take forever to cook: in fact, you can throw away the beans and eat the pan.

• Always preboil red beans in fresh water for 10 minutes or so before you start to cook them. Throw away the water and start again using cold water. This is true particularly for red kidney beans, but I apply it to any red bean.

preparing dressings

Although this book isn't a compendium of every salad and every dressing ever known, there are a few hobby-horses I would like to put over the jumps.

• Why on earth does anyone ever make a dressing in a bottle – or keep it for later? The simplest way to make a vinaigrette is to put the ingredients in the salad bowl and beat them with a fork. Put the leaves on top, toss them with your hands (clean I would assume) or, if you're very dainty, a couple of spoons. Hands are kinder, and you can make sure every leaf is lightly covered with oil. It takes absolutely no time, and you don't have unpleasant bottles of dregs lurking about in the refrigerator.

• Some salads with very tender leaves, like lamb's lettuce or baby rocket, you might like to dress at the last minute, perhaps

even having your guests add their own dressing. My solution is to mix it and put it in a small jug so you can pour it properly.

• So you won't need any screw-top jars – except if you're going on a picnic, when you could take the dressing separately the in a jar and dress just before serving.

• Italy provides the best idea of all. Like sensible people they have the oil, vinegar, salt and pepper on the table for people to dress the salad themselves. For an Italian salad, it always seems to work best like this anyway. The order is salt, then vinegar, then oil, tossing between each addition. Then pepper, but if you're in a restaurant, they may not trust you with the pepper grinder – you obviously have to be a sturdy Italian waiter with strong biceps and much charm in order to wield that pepper cudgel.

garlic in dressings

When garlic first dawned on the palates of non-Mediterranean people, we were advised to rub the (wooden) salad bowl with it, so our taste-buds wouldn't get too much of a fright and our breath wouldn't offend. Presumably, the salad bowl soon started to smell of stale garlic.

However, I do think you can overdo garlic in salad dressings, especially at the end of the season, when garlic is very strong and peppery. So that's my rule: late in the season, I use about 1 garlic clove in a salad for 4 people, crushed to a paste with

a pinch of salt, before stirring in the other dressing ingredients. In spring, when it's mild and sweet, I use as many as I like.

In fact, spring garlic sliced into a bowl of oil makes a great dip. Cut it across the top into thin slices to produce a beautiful mosaic pattern. Put in a small bowl, cover with oil, sprinkle a few drops of balsamic vinegar on top, followed by sea salt flakes and cracked black pepper. Let infuse for 30 minutes or so before using it as a dip for raw or blanched vegetables – a sort of *pinzimonio balsamico*.

the vinaigrette family

Vinaigrette can be a simple thing – just oil, vinegar or other acidulator such as lime or lemon juice, plus salt and freshly ground black pepper. You can add lots of other things to ring the changes, but in my opinion this simple mixture can't be beaten. I think the oil should be as good as you can find, and the vinegar as little as possible. The secret is in the ratio of oil to vinegar. I like the ratio of 6 parts oil to 1 part vinegar, but this can be a matter of taste. I find you can use more if the vinegar is replaced by lemon juice. However, remember, if you have to add sugar, you've probably used too much vinegar.

vinaigrette

6 tablespoons extra virgin olive oil
1 tablespoon white wine vinegar
sea salt and freshly ground black pepper
makes about 125 ml

Put the oil, vinegar, salt and pepper in a salad bowl and beat with a fork or small whisk.

variations

• Add 1 teaspoon Dijon mustard and beat well. The mustard helps form an emulsion.

• Use harissa paste instead of mustard.

• Crush the garlic with a pinch of salt to form a paste.

• I like to use Japanese rice vinegar, which gives a mild, smooth taste. You can also substitute red wine vinegar, sherry vinegar, cider vinegar or others.

• Use freshly squeezed lime or lemon juice instead of vinegar.

• Instead of extra virgin, use 2 tablespoons mild virgin olive oil and 3 tablespoons nut oil such as walnut, hazelnut or macadamia (page 14). Nut oils turn rancid very quickly, so buy small quantities, keep in the refrigerator and use quickly (keep nuts there too).

• Heat the vinaigrette in a small saucepan over a gentle heat until just warm, then pour over the salad.

• One of the nicest dressings of all is just a sprinkle of the very best quality extra virgin olive oil.

• Amazingly, a simple sprinkling of lemon juice or a mild vinegar is a great dressing for some salads such as tomatoes.

blue cheese dressing

250 g dolcellate, Gorgonzola or other blue cheese, crumbled
6 tablespoons extra virgin olive oil
2 tablespoons white wine vinegar
sea salt and freshly ground black pepper
makes about 125 ml

To make the dressing, put the crumbled cheese in a bowl and crush with a fork. Add 2 tablespoons of the olive oil and mash until creamy, adding the remaining olive oil and the vinegar as you go. If the end result is too thick, beat in a little hot water until the mixture is loose and creamy. Add salt and pepper to taste – take care with the salt, because blue cheese is already quite salty.

The dressing will thicken on standing, so you may have beat it again before serving (or you can add a little water to thin it down).

italian dressing

In many Italian restaurants, especially in Italy, you will see a 'cruet' of oil and vinegar (below) or just bottles of vinegar and oil, usually from the local area. You dress your salad to taste. First the salt, then vinegar, then the oil.

reduced balsamic vinegar

Sydney food writer Louise Pickford reduces cheap balsamic vinegar to produce a thick dressing, used in drops.

300 ml balsamic vinegar
makes 100 ml

Put the vinegar in a small saucepan, bring to the boil, then simmer gently until it is reduced by two-thirds and is the consistency of thick syrup. Let cool, then store in a clean bottle. The result can be used in drops as a seasoning.

the mayonnaise family

The key to making mayonnaise is to have all the ingredients at room temperature and to add the oil a few drops at a time at first, then more quickly, but not in a continuous stream as many books advise. The emulsion needs time to absorb the oil, so don't overtax it. Don't use all olive oil (unless you're making aïoli) – the flavour is too strong. Use a light oil such as sunflower, but good quality: don't use those labelled just 'vegetable oil', because they have usually been heat-extracted (cold-pressed is healthier for you).

I prefer a food processor to make mayonnaise but, if you're a purist, by all means make it by hand.

classic mayonnaise

2 egg yolks, at room temperature

1 whole egg (if making in a food processor)

2 teaspoons Dijon mustard

a large pinch of salt

2 teaspoons freshly squeezed lemon juice or white wine vinegar

250 ml good-quality sunflower, safflower or peanut oil (not corn oil)

125 ml virgin olive oil

makes about 500 ml

If making in a food processor, put the egg yolks, whole egg, mustard, salt and lemon juice in the bowl and blend until pale. If making by hand, omit the whole egg. Gradually add the oil, a few drops at a time at first, then more quickly, but in stages, leaving a few seconds between additions to allow the eggs to 'digest' the oil. When all the oil has been added, if the mixture is too thick, add 1 tablespoon warm water. Serve immediately, or press clingfilm over

the surface to prevent a skin from forming. It may be refrigerated for up to 3 days.

aïoli

An unctuous garlic mayonnaise served with Provençal dishes such as Le Grand Aïoli on page 48. Crush 4 garlic cloves and put in a food processor at the same time as the eggs. Proceed as in the main recipe, using all olive oil. In spring, you can use more garlic than later in the season.

rouille aïoli

Add 1 tablespoon harissa paste at the end of the recipe to make a quick rouille with a North African accent.

potato salad dressing

200 ml light cream

½ recipe Classic Mayonnaise (left)

1 tablespoon Dijon mustard

makes about 375 ml

Stir the cream into the mayonnaise to thin it a little, then stir in the mustard. This should only be done with homemade mayonnaise. Alternatively, omit the cream and use a whole recipe of mayonnaise.

thousand island dressing

An American classic, good with cold cuts.

200 ml Classic Mayonnaise (left)

50 ml low-fat yoghurt

3 tablespoons chilli sauce

½ green pepper, finely chopped

½ red pepper, roasted and finely chopped

1 teaspoon finely grated onion

makes about 500 ml

Put the mayonnaise and yoghurt into a bowl. Add the chilli sauce, peppers and onion and stir well. Serve immediately or cover and refrigerate for up to 8 hours.

green goddess dressing

Another great American dressing.

500 ml Classic Mayonnaise (left)

8 canned anchovy fillets, drained and mashed with a fork

2 spring onions, green and white, chopped

a bunch of chives, scissor-snipped

a handful of parsley, chopped

2 tablespoons chopped fresh tarragon

4 tablespoons tarragon vinegar

makes about 750 ml

Put all the ingredients in a bowl and stir well. Serve immediately or cover and refrigerate for up to 8 hours.

variation

Put 250 ml mayonnaise in a food processor. Add 4 canned anchovies, salt, pepper, 2 tablespoons each of tarragon, parsley and chives, 1 tablespoon lemon juice and 3 tablespoons vinegar. Process until smooth.

the pesto family

Although in Italy, pesto is only served with pasta, the rest of the world has fallen in love with it. It makes a delicious dressing for many kinds of salad – potato, tomato, chickpeas and beans – or stirred through rice or couscous with extra herbs.

basil pesto

4 tablespoons pine nuts

4 garlic cloves, crushed

1 teaspoon sea salt

a large double handful of basil leaves

25 g freshly grated Parmesan cheese

125 ml extra virgin olive oil, or to taste

makes about 250 ml

Put the pine nuts in a dry frying pan and fry gently and quickly until golden (about 30 seconds). They burn very easily, so don't leave them. Let cool. Transfer to a food processor or blender, add the garlic, salt and basil and purée to a paste. Add the Parmesan, blend again, then add the oil and blend again until smooth. Add extra oil if you want a looser texture.

parsley pesto

A much milder version using parsley instead of basil when the basil has not yet reached its full summer flavour, or all you have is the infant supermarket kind. Try almonds instead of walnuts in this pesto.

rocket pesto

Use half parsley and half rocket leaves.

red pesto

Instead of basil, use 250 g sun-dried tomatoes bottled in olive oil, but drained. A teaspoon of harissa paste lifts the flavour even further.

coriander pesto

Use coriander leaves instead of basil, peanut or sunflower oil instead of olive, 1 garlic clove, a squeeze of lemon or lime juice, and (optional) grated fresh ginger.

asian dressings

south-east asian dressings

Although South-east Asia has created dozens of dressings, those without oil appeal to me most. They include salt, sour, sweet and hot elements, and cooks add a little more of one or less of another according to their taste, traditions and the flavour and texture of what they're dressing. In Vietnam especially, salt components don't appear on the table, so it's up to the cook to decide. The one element the diners are trusted to add to taste is chilli. That said, in some Thai restaurants, it's common with some dishes (not usually salads) to be given a 'cruet' set of grated palm sugar, crushed dried chillies, chillies in vinegar and chillies in fish sauce. Fire!

vietnamese chilli-lime dressing

You will notice that there is quite a lot of brown sugar in this one, because of the large quantity of chilli and ginger. Before the Portuguese took chillies to Asia, pepper and ginger alone satisfied the appetite for hot, spicy tastes. Now you can't think of Asia without chillies. Ground peanuts are often used as a topping.

6 tablespoons lime juice, 2–3 limes

1 tablespoon fish sauce

2 tablespoons brown sugar

2 chillies, deseeded and finely chopped

1 garlic clove, crushed

3 cm fresh ginger, peeled and grated

makes about 200 ml

Put all the ingredients in a bowl and beat well until the sugar has dissolved.

thai fresh chilli dressing

4 tablespoons lime juice

2 tablespoons fish sauce

2 chillies, deseeded and chopped

makes about 125 ml

Put the lime juice, fish sauce and chillies in a bowl and stir.

spicy thai dressing

4 tablespoons fish sauce

freshly squeezed juice of 1 lemon or 2 limes

2 teaspoons brown sugar

2 tablespoons red Thai curry paste

makes about 125 ml

Put the fish sauce, lime or lemon juice, sugar and curry paste in a bowl and beat with a fork.

sesame oil dressing

3 cm fresh ginger, peeled and sliced

3 spring onions, chopped

1 red chilli, deseeded and chopped

1 tablespoon peppercorns, preferably Szechuan

200 ml peanut oil

4 tablespoons sesame oil

makes about 375 ml

Put the ginger, spring onions, chilli and peppercorns in a small blender and pulse to chop. Put the peanut and sesame oils in a saucepan and heat until hot but not smoking. Remove from the heat, add the flavourings, stir, cover with a lid, let cool, then strain. Serve tossed through blanched vegetables, chicken or noodle salads.

lime dressing

1 tablespoon fish sauce

freshly squeezed juice of 1 lime

1 teaspoon brown sugar

makes about 4 tablespoons

Mix in a small bowl and serve as a dipping sauce, or sprinkled over a salad.

peanut sauce

250 g shelled raw peanuts

2 red chillies, deseeded and thinly sliced

2 bird's eye chillies, deseeded and thinly sliced

1 onion, finely chopped

1 garlic clove, crushed

1 teaspoon sea salt

2 teaspoons brown sugar

200 ml canned coconut milk

serves 4–8

Toast the peanuts in a dry frying pan. Transfer to a clean, dry tea towel, rub off the skins, then put the nuts in a blender. Grind to a coarse meal, then add the chillies, onion, garlic, salt, sugar and coconut milk. Blend to a purée, then

transfer to a saucepan and cook, stirring, until thickened. When ready to serve, thin with water to a pourable consistency.

japanese dressings

Japanese salads usually involve just one or two ingredients, simply dressed, served in small quantities, beautifully arranged in small bowls, heaped in a mountain shape.

sambai-zu

This is a popular everyday Japanese salad dressing, used in many homes. Sweet, salty and sour.

3 tablespoons rice vinegar

1 teaspoon tamari soy sauce

1 tablespoon white sugar

a pinch of salt

makes about 6 tablespoons

Put all the ingredients in a bowl and beat with a fork. Spoon over the salad.

kimi-zu

A Japanese version of mayonnaise.

2 egg yolks

1/2 teaspoon salt

1 1/2 tablespoons white sugar

1/2 teaspoon cornflour

4 tablespoons dashi stock*

2 tablespoons rice vinegar

makes about 200 ml

Put the egg yolks in a heatproof bowl set over a saucepan of simmering water. Don't let the base of the bowl touch the water. Whisk well, then beat in the salt, sugar and cornflour. Gradually stir in the dashi and vinegar. Continue simmering, stirring until thickened. The cornflour will stop it curdling, but don't let it boil.

nihai-zu

A dressing for shellfish and fish salads, like the Crab and Cucumber Salad on page 75.

3 tablespoons white rice vinegar

2 tablespoons tamari soy sauce

a pinch of salt

makes about 5 tablespoons

Put all the ingredients in a bowl and whisk with a fork. Spoon over the salad.

goma-zu

Sesame seed dressing, good for vegetables.

4 tablespoons black sesame seeds

1 tablespoon sugar

2 tablespoons tamari soy sauce

1 tablespoon sake

2 tablespoons rice vinegar

makes 200 ml

Toast the sesame seeds in a dry frying pan over low heat until aromatic. Using a mortar and pestle, grind to a powder. Add the sugar and grind again, then stir in the soy sauce, sake and vinegar. If preferred, add 1 tablespoon water or dashi.

ponzu sauce

This fashionable dressing can be difficult to make because yuzu fruit (a kind of citrus fruit) is rare outside Japan. The juice is sometimes available in specialist stores, or can be ordered.

grated zest and juice of 1 yuzu or small blood orange (or Seville)

tamari soy sauce

Put the zest and juice in a bowl, then stir in an equal quantity of soy sauce.

Most common Asian ingredients are now available in larger supermarkets. Japanese ingredients, such as powdered dashi, can be found near the sushi ingredients. Chinese and other Asian markets also sell it in liquid concentrate form.

things on top

four ways with croutons

The traditional way to prepare croutons is to cut thick slices of bread, remove the crusts, then cut the remainder into cubes (day-old bread is best). Heat butter or butter and oil in a frying pan, add the cubes and sauté until golden on all sides. I always find that it's too easy to burn them this way.

Alternatively, you put the cubes into a roasting tin, sprinkle with oil, toss to coat, then cook in a preheated oven at 200°C (400°F) Gas 6 until golden.

A friend of mine toasts the slices in a toaster until pale gold, then cuts the slices into cubes and fries them in just a little butter and oil until golden.

I always find that my croutons squash into flat squares, not tidy cubes. So I prefer them more freeform, rough and ready. I tear good Italian bread into bits, heat a little olive oil in a frying pan and sauté until golden on most sides. It is a little more rustic, but equally delicious. A garlic clove squashed into the cooking oil makes them even better. However, if you prefer traditional, don't let me lead you astray.

salt, sweet and sour

pancetta and bacon

There's nothing more delicious than salty, smoky ham or crispy bacon added to a salad. I like cubed unsmoked pancetta, streaky bacon, bacon lardons, thinly sliced smoked pancetta, or Italian Parma ham in any guise. It goes very well with creamy things like avocado and some cheese.

For crisp bacon, it's best to choose the fatty end of the flitch, known in Britain as 'streaky'. Because in some parts of the world people now think bacon is a chunk of pig with no fat, I would suggest that Italian pancetta is the best option. I buy the smoked kind, either in the piece so I can cut it into cubes, or I ask the shopkeeper to cut it as fine as paper – nothing is as crisp and delicious. However, even supermarkets now sell little square tubs of cubetti – pancetta ready cut into squares. Or you can cut them yourself into lardons (2 cm long square strips).

anchovies

Anchovy is my favourite salty flavour, along with fish sauce. I use the dry-salted kind, preferably taken from a big can, packed as a wheel, noses in the middle, from an old-fashioned Greek or Italian deli. You have to wash, skin and bone them yourself. Since such stores are a dying breed, I am usually forced to use the canned or bottled kind. Use them as fillets, or mash them into the dressing (and don't use any more salt in the salad until you've tasted it).

Anchovies act much as soy or fish sauce do in Asian cooking – as a salt flavour, but a more interesting, smoky kind of salt.

sugar

In South-east Asian salads, palm sugar is used to balance the fire of chillies. If you can't find it, use brown instead – I think if you're going to use sugar, it should have more oomph than ordinary white sugar. I don't think you should have to use it in vinaigrettes at all – if you do, you've used too much vinegar.

lemon zest and lime zest

An unbeatable addition to all sorts of foods. Think of lime added to tropical flavours and lemon to more temperature ones. Remove the zest in shreds or grate it finely. Whatever you use, invest in a good zester, one that doesn't include the bitter white pith. Even more important is to choose unwaxed fruit, or to wash off the wax with warm water (if it's too hot, it will release the essential oils and you'll lose some of the flavour).

capers and caperberries

These two ingredients come from a Mediterranean wall plant, a little like a nasturtium. Capers (the buds) and their cousins caperberries (the berries) are one of those love-them-or-hate-them flavours— a mixture of salt and vinegar that appeals to a grown-up palate, just like olives, which you hate when you're a child, but learn to love later.

olives

Black or green, pitted or not, dry-cured, with flavourings such as herbs, garlic, chillies or pepper, or stuffed (please not!) with pimentos. I always prefer them with the pits in – in the belief that they taste so much better. If the recipe needs pitted ones, pit them yourself. I like best-quality olives, like Kalamata from Greece, Niçoise from the south of France, and anything Italian.

toasted nuts and seeds, and nut or seed oils

Toasted nuts or seeds are a wonderful addition to a salad. But almost any nut or seed will be improved by being lightly toasted in a dry frying pan before use. Think of pine nuts, and how amazingly good they taste after this treatment.

The Vietnamese make masterly salads, and you often find toasted peanuts sprinkled over them to give them extra crunch (and protein too, which is important if you are a vegetarian).

When I'm putting nuts into salads – apart from pine nuts – I sometimes like to complement them with a dash of their own oil. However, as I've said elsewhere, nut and seed oils deteriorate very fast, so buy them in small bottles and use them quickly. I keep them in the refrigerator after they've been opened, though some oil purists disapprove of this.

So, match macadamias to macadamia oil, pumpkin seeds to (a few drops only) of beautiful green pumpkin seed oil, hazelnuts with their oil, walnuts with theirs, sesame seeds with a few drops of toasted sesame oil. But, if you don't have the required nut oil, don't worry – just use good olive oil and the toasted nut (toasted in the oven or in a frying pan). And if you haven't yet discovered avocado oil, start today – it's good for salad, and wonderful for cooking.

crisp fried things

I don't know why, but the human palate just loves crispy, crunchy things. Yes, I know celery and apples fall into that category, but add a little bit of oil and perhaps a dash of salt, and suddenly we are devoted to the crispy texture.

vegetable crisps

Thinly slice onions, shallots, garlic, pumpkin or parsnips, using a mandoline or vegetable peeler. Fill a wok or deep-fryer one-third full of peanut oil or other mild-flavoured oil (or to the manufacturer's recommended level).

Heat the oil to about 190°C (375°F) or to the manufacturer's recommended temperature. Test using an inexpensive sugar thermometer, or drop in a cube of bread – it should turn golden brown in about 30–40 seconds.

Add the sliced vegetables in batches (not too many at a time) and cook on both sides until crisp and golden. Drain on crumpled kitchen paper. If you want to keep them warm, do so in a low oven.

deep-fried herbs

Herb leaves such as parsley, sage, curry leaves and others are delicious fried to a crisp, either in a wok or deep-fryer as above, or shallow-fried in a frying pan using olive oil or a mixture of butter and oil.

asian crispy things

Asian supermarkets sell interesting crispy things that are wonderful for topping all kinds of dishes. I like Vietnamese fried shallots, onions or garlic; Asian dried shrimp, which can be used as is, or ground to a powder and toasted some more. Japanese bonito flakes, that are used in making dashi stock, also have good salady uses.

herb and spice oils

You can buy herb oils and chilli oils, but I much prefer to make them myself.

basil oil

To make basil oil, put a large handful of basil in a food processor and add at least 250 ml olive oil. Blend, set aside for 30 minutes or overnight in the refrigerator, then strain into a clean bottle. Other herbs, such as parsley, may be used instead.

chilli oil

To make chilli oil, put a few fresh or dried chillies in a small bottle of oil. Let steep for a few hours or up to 1 day, then taste. If the oil is spicy enough for you, strain out the chillies, return the oil to the bottle and seal. If not, let steep longer, to taste.

leaves

green salad

In America, this salad is known as 'mesclun' (from the same origin as the word 'miscellaneous'). In Italian, it's *insalata di campo*—little salad of the fields. Choose a combination of leaves – some crisp, some bitter, some peppery, some soft – and sprigs of scented herbs. The perfection of the dressing is what's important. My view is that the oil must be as marvellous as possible and the vinegar as little as possible. I prefer it without mustard or garlic, but please

Wash the leaves as necessary and dry in a salad spinner. Put into plastic bags or wrap in dry tea towels and chill for at least 30 minutes to crisp the leaves. (If washing soft leaves like rocket, do it at the last minute, otherwise they will go mushy – thankfully, my supermarket sells them in bags, already washed and dried.)

If using garlic, put it on a board with a pinch of sea salt and crush thoroughly with the back of a heavy knife (use a garlic crusher if you must, but I think the texture is better this way). Transfer to a salad bowl, add the olive oil, vinegar, mustard, if using, and pepper, then beat with a fork or small whisk. Add extra salt and pepper, to taste.

When ready to serve, add the leaves and, using your hands, turn them gently in the dressing until lightly coated. (I prefer to use my hands, so as not to bruise the leaves and to make sure every one is well coated.) Alternatively, if you have used a large proportion of soft leaves, serve the salad undressed, with the dressing in a small jug. The salad can then be dressed by your guests just before eating.

note

A few tablespoons of dressing is plenty for a salad of this size – too much will spoil it. I also prefer the vinegar to be as gentle as possible. (White rice vinegar is my current favourite, but I also like sherry vinegar.)

salad forks

Do you remember the scene in *Pretty Woman* when Hector Elizondo teaches Julia Roberts which fork to use? In modern cutlery sets, you are expected to use the small fork for salads, but the Victorians had a special piece of cutlery for everything. Lettuce knives were never sharp, because you weren't supposed to cut the delicate leaves (they were always supposed to be torn into bite-sized pieces). In any case, you never used the knife. Salad forks on the other hand, had five tines, the outer ones were always wider, so they wouldn't damage the leaves. You can still buy these pretty forks in antique shops.

your choice of:

crisp leaves, such as Little Gem

soft leaves, such as oak leaf lettuce

peppery leaves, such as watercress or nasturtium leaves or flowers

bitter leaves, such as dandelion or chicory

rocket and wild rocket

soft herb sprigs, such as fennel, parsley or basil

dressing

½ garlic clove (optional)

a pinch of sea salt flakes

6 parts extra virgin olive oil

1 part vinegar, such as cider, white rice, sherry, white wine or red wine

1 teaspoon Dijon mustard (optional)

freshly ground black pepper

serves 4–6

caesar salad

This is probably the most famous salad in the world and the perfect combination of salty, crispy crunch. It seems to have been around forever, but not so – it was invented by Italian chef Caesar Cardini in Tijuana, Mexico, in 1924. Note that this recipe serves one person – just multiply the ingredients to serve more people.

1 egg, preferably free range and organic

6 smallest leaves of cos lettuce (a young cos, not Little Gem)

1/2 tablespoon freshly squeezed lemon juice, plus 1 lemon cut into wedges, to serve (optional)

2 tablespoons extra virgin olive oil

3–4 canned anchovy fillets, rinsed and drained

Parmesan cheese, at room temperature, shaved into curls with a vegetable peeler

sea salt and freshly ground black pepper

croutons

1 thick slice crusty white bread or challah bread

2 tablespoons oil and/or butter, for cooking

1 garlic clove, crushed

serves 1

To cook the egg, put it in a small saucepan and bring to the boil. Reduce the heat and simmer for 4–5 minutes. Remove from the heat and cover with cold water to stop it cooking further. Let cool a little, then peel. Cut into quarters just before serving.

To make the croutons, tear the bread into bite-sized chunks, brush with oil or butter and rub with the garlic. Cook on a preheated stove-top grill pan until crisply golden and barred with brown. Alternatively, follow one of the methods on page 12.

Put the lettuce into a large bowl and sprinkle with salt and pepper, add the lemon juice and toss with your hands. Finally, sprinkle with olive oil and toss again.

Put the croutons into a bowl and put the dressed leaves on top. Add the anchovies, egg and Parmesan, sprinkle with pepper and serve with lemon wedges, if using.

notes

• Of course, the croutons were traditionally made of sliced bread cut into cubes, and I love them made this way. Just for a change, however, I've made them freeform, so you get lots of crisp, crunchy edges. Be classic if you prefer.

• Originally, the salad used a one-minute egg – coddled, rather than boiled – so that the egg became part of the dressing. These days, some people are nervous about eggs, so I have done it my favourite way – simmered for 4–5 minutes after the water has come to the boil. The white will be set, but the yolk still soft and creamy.

chicory with chorizo

Salads don't have to be complicated. This one is very simple –
shown here as a starter, though you can easily increase the
quantities and serve as a side salad with pasta or other dishes.
Chicory (Belgian endive or witloof) has a juicy but bitter leaf. Bitter
seems to go very well with a little spice – from Dijon mustard, or
from the smoky paprika flavour of the chorizo. There are different
kinds of chorizo available – the ones you need are the small, whole,
slightly dried sausages, about 8 cm long and perhaps 2 cm in
diameter, sold in strings. The ones with white strings are known
as sweet, the ones with red are spicy (very).

Put the chorizo on a chopping board and slice them very thinly with a sharp knife. Heat the
olive oil in a frying pan, then add the chorizo slices. Fry until brown on one side, then turn
them over and brown the other side. Remove from the heat.

Make the vinaigrette in a salad bowl. Cut the root end off the chicory, pull the leaves apart
and add them to the bowl. Toss well, then pile onto 4 salad plates. Add the chorizo, then
drizzle any of the spicy red oil from the pan over the top.

note

When choosing chicory, remember the paler they are, the less bitter they will be – the
bitterness is bleached out by blanching under cover.

variation

Chicory is also very good with Blue Cheese Dressing (pages 21, 42).

2 small sweet chorizo sausages
(not the larger chorizo, sold in slices
like salami)

2 tablespoons olive oil

4–6 heads of chicory, pink, white or
both, as pale as possible

1 recipe Vinaigrette with Dijon
Mustard (page 21)

serves 4

il cicorino con l'aglio

Gabriella, who is the art director of this book, is from Milan, and this is her favourite salad. In Italy, the leaves are sold in supermarkets, ready-shredded in plastic containers. It can be difficult to find this particular variety at some times of the year, and in some areas. It helps if you remember it as one of the firm-leaf varieties of escarole, also known as chicory or endive, according to where you live. It is slightly bitter in taste, so look for something with the same characteristics. *Il cicorino* is the traditional accompaniment to char-grilled steak – *tagliata*. Remember, Italians taste and add ingredients to their salad dressings as needed, since every oil, every vinegar – even salt – is different.

Remove the hard cicorino stalks, if any, and arrange the leaves one on top of the other on a wooden board. Finely slice them into a 'chiffonade'.

Put the garlic, salt and vinegar into a small bowl and beat with a fork. Beat in the olive oil. Taste, and add pepper, or extra salt, vinegar, or oil, beating as you go.

Put the cicorino in a salad bowl and trickle the dressing over the top. Toss and serve with char-grilled steak.

note

A chiffonade is a tangle of finely sliced lettuce, usually iceberg. These strong escarole leaves are one of the few salad leaves you can cut in this way – most leaves are better torn.

250 g cicorino (escarole-type bitter leaves)

1 garlic clove, crushed

1 tablespoon vinegar

6 tablespoons extra virgin olive oil

sea salt and freshly ground black pepper

char-grilled steak, cut into strips, to serve

serves 4

a wedge with blue

My thanks to photographer Peter Cassidy for this perfect idea for iceberg. After sneering at this old-fashioned lettuce for many a long year, I have 'found iceberg' again. I think its reputation was ruined by years of shredding, appearing in the nastiest sandwiches, ghastly buffet salads and general lettuce abuse. It's one of the few lettuces that can be cut, but don't overdo it. Serving it in a wedge is as violent as iceberg handling should be! The blue cheese dressing is one of my favourites. And, amazingly, we've found this dish makes great party fingerfood.

1 firm iceberg lettuce

blue cheese dressing

125 g dolcelatte, Gorgonzola or other blue cheese, crumbled

6 tablespoons extra virgin olive oil

2 tablespoons white wine vinegar

sea salt and freshly ground black pepper

serves 4

To make the dressing, put the crumbled cheese into a bowl. Crush it up as much as you can with a fork. Add 2 tablespoons of the olive oil and mash until creamy, adding the remaining olive oil and the vinegar as you go. If the end result is too thick, beat in a little hot water until the mixture is loose and creamy. Add salt and pepper to taste – take care with the salt, because blue cheese is already quite salty. The dressing will thicken on standing, so you may need to beat it again just before serving.

Remove the outer leaves of the iceberg and trim the stem.

Cut the lettuce into 4–8 wedges, depending on size, and cut out any thick stalk. Put it on a plate, curved side down, like a boat. Trickle the blue cheese dressing over the top.

note

The white juice that comes out of the stalk when you cut it is lettuce milk, an old-fashioned cure for insomnia.

greek horta salad

In Australia, Greek migrants arrived after World War II bearing wonderful fruits and vegetables, olive oil and a way with herbs that helped to transform our food. I bought a huge bunch of beetroot, with fresh leaves and purple stems, from my Greek greengrocer in Sydney. This is the recipe he suggested, and it's also good made with spinach, silver beet or ruby chard. I've included some baby beetroot wedges too, just because they're pretty (though the recipe then isn't literally *horta*).

Wash the beetroot leaves, then put in a wide saucepan just with the water clinging to the leaves. Bring to the boil, put the lid on tightly, lower the heat and simmer for a few minutes until the leaves are just wilted. The time will depend on the kind of leaves you've used.

Remove, cool under running water, and drain. Chill until ready to serve, still draining.

When ready to serve. Put into a wide dish and sprinkle with olive oil, then with sea salt and cracked black pepper. Serve with the lemon, which should be squeezed over just before eating.

variation

Add cooked beetroot wedges to the salad. Wash any earth off the beetroot but do not damage them. Leave the roots on. To cook the beetroot, either boil or roast. The cooking times will vary according to the size of the beetroot – test one with a skewer after about 30 minutes.

To boil, put them in a saucepan, cover with cold water, bring to the boil and simmer until almost tender. Salt the water, then simmer until done. Let cool, then slip off the skins. If small leave them whole, otherwise cut into halves or wedges.

To roast, rub the beetroot with olive oil, sprinkle with salt and cook in a preheated oven at 200°C (400°F) Gas 6 until done. Remove from the oven, let cool, then cut into wedges. I often leave the skins on the roasted version.

a huge handful of beetroot leaves (or, if unavailable, spinach, silver beet, Swiss chard or ruby chard)

a bunch of baby beetroot, about 6–8

4 tablespoons olive oil

1 lemon, quartered or cut into wedges

sea salt and freshly cracked black pepper

serves 4

vegetables
and fruit

le grand aïoli

This famous Provençal salad can be turned into the greatest al fresco meal of them all. The basis is garlic mayonnaise, served with fresh and blanched vegetables and a splendid whole poached fish. You can also serve chilled seafood and cold roast poultry or beef. This is a meal for lots of guests, however many will fit around your table. Set up outside, perhaps under a tree. Look out at the sunlight, the garden, the pool, the beach – and keep the wine cool and take hours about it.

In the morning, about 2 hours before lunch, prepare the poached fish. Make sure all the scales have been removed and trim the insides. Put the fish in a fish poacher or large baking dish, cover with stock or water, then add the garlic, onion and herbs. Bring to the boil, put the lid on tightly (or cover the dish with foil), turn off the heat and let cool.

To prepare the cooked vegetables, bring a large saucepan of water to the boil and have a large bowl of ice and water ready. Add the beans, blanch for about 2 minutes, then, using tongs, remove to a strainer and cool under the tap. Put the beans in the iced water. The method is the same for all the cooked vegetables – you are aiming for parboiled but still crisp. Sugar snaps and asparagus take about 1 minute, carrots 4–5 minutes, according to size, fennel about 3 minutes, depending on size, and onions about 1–2 minutes or until tender. Do not throw away the water between blanchings, because it all adds flavour to each addition. Finally, boil the peas for 1–2 minutes until cooked but not soft, then drain and chill.

When thoroughly chilled, drain all the cooked vegetables, then put each variety in a small bowl. Toss each one in a light vinaigrette to stop them drying out. Add chopped mint to the carrots. Cover with clingfilm and chill. Prepare all the uncooked vegetables, wash, drain and trim. Set on platters, cover with clingfilm and chill until ready to serve.

Carefully remove the fish from the cold poaching liquid and transfer to a large platter. Remove and discard the skin and dry the platter with kitchen paper. Put the lemon wedges around the fish. Set the platter and all the vegetables the table and spoon the aïoli into a big bowl. Let your guests help themselves, cut lots of crunchy bread and serve red and chilled white wines and lots of sparkling water.

1 whole fish, such as salmon

salted fish stock or water, to cover

6 garlic cloves, halved

1 onion, sliced

a bunch of herbs, such as thyme, rosemary and bay leaves

Vinaigrette (page 21)

at least 2 quantities of Aïoli (page 22)

6 lemons, cut into wedges.

your choice of chilled uncooked vegetables, such as:

cherry tomatoes, on the vine

chicory, red or white, leaves separated

spring onions

red peppers, preferably long ones, deseeded and sliced lengthways

your choice of chilled blanched vegetables, such as:

baby string beans

asparagus

sugar snap peas and/or peas

baby carrots

baby fennel

baby onions

baby artichokes

baby courgettes, halved lengthways

serves an inflatable number of feasters

avocado salad

Avocado is probably my favourite salad ingredient – so creamy and delicious it can really be used as a dressing in itself. My only rule is to scoop out the flesh with a teaspoon into round, rough balls – I see no point in cutting it into wedges, which is difficult to do and never looks tidy. I mix avocado with whatever looks good that day – prawns, crab, smoked fish, smoked chicken pulled into shreds – top it just with a few herb leaves if they're handy, grind lots of pepper over it, maybe add a squeeze of lemon juice, and eat it without any dressing. Avocado loves salty things, like seafood, smoked food – and bacon. If you have to share it with others, by all means serve it with these salad leaves and a regular dressing.

If using pancetta, cut the slices into 3–4 pieces. Heat a frying pan, brush with the 1 tablespoon olive oil, add the pancetta or pancetti (lardons) and cook at medium heat, without disturbing the pancetta, until crisp on one side. Using tongs, turn the slices over and fry until crisp and papery but not too brown. Remove and drain on kitchen paper.

Put the dressing ingredients in a salad bowl and beat with a fork or small whisk. When ready to serve, add the leaves and turn in the dressing, using your hands. Cut the avocados in half and remove the stones. Using a teaspoon, scoop out balls of avocado into the salad. Toss gently if you like (though this will send the avocado to the bottom of the bowl). Add the crispy pancetta or pancetti and serve.

note

• To test an avocado for ripeness, don't stick your thumb in it. Instead, cradle it in the palm of your hand and squeeze gently. If it just gives to the pressure, it's perfect.

• It's not true that keeping the stone in guacamole or other avocado dish will stop it going brown. However, lime juice, lemon juice or vinegar will. I prefer to add it to dishes at the very last minute so it has no chance to discolour.

6 very thin slices smoked pancetta or bacon, or about 200 g pancetti cubes

250 g salad leaves – a mixture of soft, crisp and peppery

1–2 ripe Hass avocados

1 tablespoon olive oil, for frying

dressing

6 tablespoons extra virgin olive oil

1 tablespoon cider vinegar or rice vinegar

1 garlic clove, crushed

1 teaspoon Dijon mustard

sea salt and freshly ground black pepper

serves 4

papaya ginger salsa

There are two kinds of salsa – the sauce kind and the salad kind. Both these recipes are salads, delicious served with main dishes, in tortillas, or as a bed for other ingredients as a starter. This one is terrific with fish and seafood.

Peel the peppers with a vegetable peeler, then cut off the tops and bottoms, scoop out the seeds and membranes and cut the flesh down one side. Open it out into a long rectangle. Cut the rectangle into squares, about 1 cm.

Squeeze the grated ginger through a garlic press into a serving bowl. Add the lime juice and sugar, and salt and pepper to taste. Whisk with a fork, then add the peppers and chilli. Toss gently, then add the papaya, coriander and lime zest and toss gently so as not to break up the papaya. Top with the lime wedges and serve.

1 red pepper

1 yellow pepper

1 large red chilli, deseeded and chopped

5 cm fresh ginger, peeled and grated

finely grated zest and juice of 2 unwaxed limes, plus lime wedges, to serve

1 teaspoon sugar, or to taste (optional)

1 ripe papaya, peeled, deseeded and cubed

a large handful of coriander leaves

sea salt and freshly ground black pepper

serves 4

avocado salsa

Avocado is very good with peppery ingredients as well as salty. I think this salsa is well suited to chicken dishes or even on its own, piled onto crusty bread.

Cut the onions in half lengthways (discard the green stalk on the spring onions). Peel off the outside layer, then cut them into feathery petals lengthways through the root. Slice the spring onions diagonally.

Mix the dressing ingredients in a large bowl. Add the onions, parsley, mint and chilli and toss lightly in the dressing. Using a teaspoon, scoop the avocado into the bowl and stir very gently to cover with the dressing, then serve.

2 very small red onions

4 spring onions with large bulbs

2 tablespoons coarsely chopped fresh parsley

2 tablespoons coarsely chopped fresh mint

1 green chilli, deseeded and very finely chopped

2 ripe Hass avocados, halved and stones removed

lime dressing

freshly squeezed juice of 2 limes

2 tablespoons olive oil

sea salt and freshly ground black pepper

serves 4

waldorf salad

When I first made this salad, the apples were unpeeled and cut into chunks, so eating it became rather hard work. I found this more elegant, Edwardian version in an old cookbook and have combined the two. It's good with barbecue grills – and suits pork very well, since pork and apples were made for each other. Make it with ripe Granny Smiths so they won't be too tart, or choose crisp red apples instead. The dressing is also old-fashioned, but though it seems unusual now, it's delicious. Use mayonnaise if you prefer.

3–4 Granny Smith apples

freshly squeezed juice of 1 lemon

2 celery stalks, thinly sliced

125 g walnut pieces or pecans, coarsely chopped

125 ml Classic Mayonnaise (page 22) or Lemon Cream Dressing (page 63)

To prepare the salad, cut a few slices of apple with skin for decoration, then peel and core the remainder and cut into matchstick strips, using a mandoline. Toss them in the lemon juice to stop them turning brown. Finely slice the celery, put into a bowl, add the apples and walnuts, then spoon over the sauce.

note

Mayonnaise is one of the classic dressings for Waldorf, but I must admit I prefer the Lemon Cream Dressing on page 63. It sounds unlikely, but it is incredibly light.

serves 4

fennel and mint salad

I had to include this simple salad, invented on a lovely autumn weekend staying with friends at their farmhouse in Umbria.

4 small heads of fennel, trimmed and quartered lengthways

2 small flat Italian onions (*cipolline*), or ½ mild red onion

a handful of parsley, scissor-snipped

a handful of mint, torn

sea salt and freshly ground black pepper

1 recipe Italian Dressing, made with red wine vinegar (page 21)

serves 4

Finely slice the fennel and put into a bowl. If using flat Italian onions, cut them in half put the 2 halves together. Finely slice them into half-moons. If using other onions, finely slice and chop. If they are very peppery, put them in a colander and pour boiling water over them, then drain. Add to the salad.

Sprinkle the parsley and mint over the salad and toss well. Add the Italian dressing, toss well, taste, then add more of the vinaigrette ingredients if necessary. Serve as part of an antipasti or lunch.

red salad with beetroot, red cabbage and harissa dressing

I devised this recipe one summer's day when friends were coming over for a barbecue. They were going to have a regular red coleslaw, but I had a few small beetroot that day, and the food stylist in me couldn't resist the colour combination. Crushing the cabbage and vinegar together with your hands has a miraculous effect on the cabbage, breaking its fibres and releasing its juices.

6–8 small beetroot

2–4 small whole heads of garlic, preferably pink spring garlic

olive oil, for roasting

1 small red cabbage

2 tablespoons white wine vinegar, cider vinegar or lemon juice

2 red onions or 6 spring onions

1 tablespoon umeboshi plum vinegar (page 14), or to taste (optional)

sea salt and freshly ground black pepper

2 medium red chillies, finely sliced (optional), to serve

harissa dressing

125 ml cold-pressed extra virgin olive oil

1 tablespoon harissa paste or 1 teaspoon chile oil

serves 4–6

Leave the beetroot whole and unpeeled. Cut the top off each garlic, about 1 cm from the stalk. You will be able to see all the cloves. Put the beetroot and garlic in a small baking dish, add olive oil, turn to coat on all sides, then sprinkle with salt and pepper. Put more oil into the garlic. Roast in a preheated oven at 200°C (400°F) Gas 6 for about 30–45 minutes or until the beetroot and garlic are tender (you may have to remove the beetroot first). Baste several times during cooking, spooning the oil into the garlic. When cooked, remove from the oven and cut the beetroot into 4 wedges (peel them or not, as you like).

About 15 minutes before the beetroot are cooked, cut the cabbage in quarters and remove the white cores. Cut the quarters into fine slices and put in a bowl. Sprinkle with vinegar and turn and mash the cabbage with your hands so the fibres break down a little and absorb it.

Cut the red onions into fine wedges, put in a bowl and cover with boiling water. Drain just before using. If using spring onions, just chop them coarsely, white and green.

When ready to serve, pop the roasted pulp out of 4 garlic cloves and put in a serving bowl. Add the olive oil and harissa and beat with a fork. Drain the onions, pat dry with kitchen paper, then add to the bowl. Sprinkle with umeboshi plum vinegar, if using. Add the cabbage and beetroot and toss gently.

Taste and adjust the seasoning with salt and pepper and top with the chillies, if using. Put the heads of garlic beside for people to press out the delicious flesh themselves.

spicy coleslaw

I'm not a fan of ordinary coleslaw, but I love the Indian way with salads. Their vegetables are glorious – super-organic, not irrigated into a complete lack of flavour – and their varieties are much more interesting than factory-farmed versions. I particularly love their huge, bright red winter carrots, which I hope to find in a farmers' market here soon.

Halve the onions lengthways, then slice into fine wedges, to make petals. Slice the tomatoes, removing any white core, and finely slice the carrot diagonally or into matchsticks. Halve the cucumbers lengthways, then slice diagonally. Put all the vegetables on a serving plate, cover and chill.

Put the lemon juice, salt, pepper and sugar into a bowl, stir and chill. When ready to serve, sprinkle the vegetables with the dressing, add the mint and serve.

variation

Indians don't use olive oil, but if you prefer, dress this salad with regular vinaigrette.

2 red onions

2 ripe tomatoes, such as plum

1 carrot

2 mini cucumbers, or about 20 cm regular cucumber

½ Savoy cabbage, halved, cored and finely sliced

freshly squeezed juice of 1 lemon or 2 nimbu (key limes)

sea salt and freshly ground black pepper

a pinch of caster sugar

a small bunch of mint, chopped, plus a few leaves, to serve

serves 4, with other dishes

classic coleslaw

If I didn't include a regular slaw, my sister would never forgive me. This is the salad she has forced me to make every Christmas from the beginning of time. Since she acquired a food processor, all the slicing and grating hasn't been such an onerous task, but I still prefer the vegetables to be hand-sliced.

250 ml Classic Mayonnaise (page 22)

125 ml Vinaigrette (page 20), or to taste

1 large white cabbage, thinly sliced

1 carrot, grated

1 red pepper, peeled, deseeded and chopped (optional)

a handful of parsley and chives, coarsely chopped

1 teaspoon caraway seeds (optional)

sea salt and freshly ground black pepper

variation dressing

Lemon Cream Dressing (page 63)

serves 8

To make the dressing, put the mayonnaise in a small bowl, add half the vinaigrette and beat well. Taste, then add more vinaigrette, 1 tablespoon at a time, until the taste and creaminess is right. The amount will depend on the flavour of the original dressings. Set aside.

Put all the vegetables in a bowl and mix well. Add half the dressing and toss to coat. Add more dressing until the texture pleases you (in our family we don't like too much dressing). Season to taste with caraway seeds, if using, plus salt and pepper, then cover and chill until needed. This will develop the flavours. Let return to room temperature for a few minutes, stir in the parsley and chives, then serve.

fruit and vegetables
with yoghurt dressing

Indian salads or raitas almost always include yoghurt as the main element of the dressing, with toasted spices, called the 'tempering', as the flavour note. You can use almost any crisp fruit or vegetable in this salad – vary the ingredients according to what's in season. The keynotes are crisp, sweet and spicy.

To make the dressing, put the ajwain, mustard seeds and chilli in a dry frying pan and toast over medium heat until aromatic. Transfer to a small bowl and let cool. Add the salt and sugar, then grate the ginger and squeeze the gratings into the bowl. Stir in the yoghurt and set aside.

Put the cashew nuts into the same pan and toast over medium heat until golden. Do not let burn. Remove from the heat, transfer to a small bowl and let cool. When cool, chop coarsely with a knife.

Put the lettuce wedges onto a plate, add the grapes, pomelo pieces, if using, grapes, radishes, cucumber and ginger. Spoon over the dressing – sparingly – don't drown it. Then sprinkle with the cashew nuts, coconut, and coriander or methi leaves, if using.

note

Methi are the leaves of the fenugreek plant – the seeds are the spice that makes curry powder smell of curry. The leaves are used as a green vegetable in Indian cooking, but when I can get them, I also like just a few fresh sprigs in salads. They give a very faint and fascinating scent of curry to the salad.

4 tablespoons cashew nuts

4 small crisp lettuces, cut into wedges or torn into pieces

6 segments pomelo or grapefruit (preferably pink), membranes removed, segments pulled into 2–3 pieces (optional)

12 large red or white grapes, or both, halved lengthways and deseeded

6 red radishes, finely sliced on a mandoline

1 mini cucumber, halved lengthways, deseeded and finely sliced on a mandoline

3 cm fresh ginger, peeled and finely sliced into thin slivers on a mandoline (julienne blade)

4 tablespoons flaked coconut, soaked in water if desiccated (optional)

sprigs of coriander or methi leaves (optional)

yoghurt dressing

a pinch of lovage (ajwain) seeds (optional)

1 teaspoon mustard seeds

a pinch of crushed chillies

1/2 teaspoon salt

1/2 teaspoon sugar

3 cm fresh ginger, peeled

250 ml plain yoghurt

serves 4

classic potato salad

I have always been mystified by the dressing on my mother's potato salad, which she made in quantity for local farmers' meetings. In those days, the only oils for cooking were dripping and butter. So what did she use? My sister came to the rescue …

Put the potatoes in a large saucepan, cover with cold water, add a large pinch of salt and bring to the boil over medium heat. Reduce the heat immediately and simmer gently until done (potatoes should always be cooked gently) – they should be cooked but still firm.

Drain. As soon as they are cool enough to touch, peel them – hold them in a dry cloth and pull off the skins with the back of a dinner knife. Slice them thickly and put in a salad bowl. Season with plenty of salt and pepper, then add the onions.

To make the dressing, put the salt, pepper and lemon juice into a bowl, stir to dissolve the salt, then gradually pour in the cream, stirring constantly. This dressing must be used immediately. Alternatively, use the traditional dressing ingredients, mixed well.

While still warm, pour the dressing over the potatoes and stir carefully, so each piece is coated with the dressing. Gently fold in the boiled eggs. Top with the herbs or spring onions and serve. Potato salad is nicer when cool, not chilled, so if you've had to refrigerate it, let it return to room temperature first.

1 kg potatoes, either medium or small waxy salad potatoes, unpeeled

2 mild onions, finely sliced into rings

6 hard-boiled eggs, chopped

salt and freshly ground white pepper

lemon cream dressing

freshly squeezed juice of 1 lemon

250 ml double cream

sea salt and white pepper

traditional dressing (optional)

1 recipe Classic Mayonnaise (page 22)

175 ml milk

to serve

a large bunch of parsley, chopped

a small bunch of mint, chopped

a handful of chives, scissor-snipped

4 spring onions, thinly sliced

serves 6

indian potato salad

On the other hand, the Indian variety of this comforting salad is spicy, crunchy and wonderfully interesting. Add extra lime juice to taste. The spice mixes may be changed to suit your taste.

Put the oil in a pan, add the mustard and cumin seeds, cinnamon, chilli and cardamom. Stir-fry until aromatic, then stir in the turmeric. Add the potatoes, salt and pepper and stir-fry for about 2 minutes. Add 250 ml water and boil until the liquid has evaporated and the potatoes are tender – add more water if necessary.

Sprinkle half the chopped onions over the top and add the coriander. Put the oil in a frying pan, add the remaining onion and the garlic and fry until golden brown. Pour the contents of the pan, and the oil, over the potatoes and toss to coat. Top with the torn coriander and serve. Let your guests squeeze juice over the salad to their own taste.

4 tablespoons peanut oil or ghee

1 tablespoon mustard seeds

1/2 tablespoon cumin seeds

1/2 cinnamon stick, crushed

1 dried red chilli, crushed

6 cardamom pods, crushed

1 teaspoon turmeric

500 g potatoes, cut into chunks

2 red onions, chopped

4 tablespoons peanut oil or ghee

1 garlic clove, crushed

a handful of coriander, torn

salt and freshly ground black pepper

serves 4

big greek salad

1 iceberg lettuce, quartered and torn apart

about 250 g feta cheese, crumbled into big pieces, or cut into cubes

about 200 g Kalamata olives

2 red onions, halved, then sliced into petals

2 mini cucumbers, halved lengthways, then thinly sliced diagonally

4 big ripe red tomatoes, cut into chunks

8 anchovy fillets, or to taste

a few sprigs of oregano, torn

a few sprigs of mint, torn

greek dressing

6 tablespoons extra virgin olive oil, preferably Greek

2 tablespoons freshly squeezed lemon juice

sea salt and freshly ground black pepper

serves 4

Greek salads are so much part of the easy, Mediterranean style of eating – a bit of crisp, a bit of fiery, a few baby herbs, some vinegary olives (and Greece produces some of the best) and salty anchovies. I used to live in Melbourne, the second biggest Greek city in the world, and I remember marvellous lunches where we snacked on a communal salad like this one as we waited for the best efforts of chefs from Kalymnos, the home island of many Australian Greek families. I love proper Kalamata olives, but unpitted, because they have more flavour – warn your guests in case they're not expecting them.

Put the lettuce in a big bowl. Add the cheese, olives, onions, cucumbers and tomatoes.

To make the dressing, put the olive oil, lemon juice, salt and pepper in a jug or bowl and beat with a fork, then pour over the salad. You can also sprinkle them onto the salad separately.

Top with the anchovies, oregano and mint, and serve.

notes

• Iceberg is one of the few lettuces than can bear to be sliced. Slice it if you wish, but I like big chunky bits.

• My favourite thing in a Greek salad is the salted anchovies, so I have extra. Greek stalls in the markets sell them in big cans – wheels of whole fish, arranged nose to tail. You rinse and fillet them yourself. If you don't have a Greek deli, use canned.

italian grilled pepper salad

A beautiful, delicious, simple salad based on the classic Insalata Caprese. If you find yourself without the most important ingredient for this salad (the very best, ripest, most flavourful tomatoes), peppers are a great solution. This salad comes from my cousin, who lives outside Naples – we have driven along country roads, buying mozzarella from the farmers and collecting rocket from the roadside verges (and peppers and tomatoes grown in local gardens).

Put the whole peppers under a hot grill, on a barbecue, or over the flame of a gas stove. Cook on all sides until charred. Remove from the heat, transfer to a saucepan and put on the lid (this will help steam off the skins). When cool, drain the juices into a small bowl.

Scrape off and discard the charred skins. Cut the peppers in half lengthways and scrape out and discard the seeds and membranes, adding any juices to the bowl.

To make the dressing, put 2 tablespoons of the juices into another bowl with the olive oil. Beat with a fork. Add salt and pepper to taste, and extra pepper juice if you like. (Keep any extra juice for another use.)

When ready to assemble the salad, tear the mozzarellas apart into big shreds – about 4 pieces each – and put on 4 chilled plates. Add a handful of rocket and 2 pepper halves to each plate. Sprinkle with the olive oil, then add a few drops of balsamic, if using, to each serving. Sprinkle with sea salt flakes and cracked pepper and serve.

notes

• Please don't slather the balsamic over the salad. Use it as a seasoning, not a dressing.

• The best mozzarella is made from buffalo milk and comes from Campania around Naples. If you don't have any buffaloes handy, any good-quality fresh mozzarella may be used. Just don't cut it – tear it apart, so it separates along its natural grain.

• There are several different kinds of rocket. In my garden, I have four – in my refrigerator, I have two. Supermarkets sell the round-leafed seedling kind, and also the variety with jagged leaves called wild rocket. Around Naples it does grow wild along country roads, where the locals gather it in season. You can try growing a few seeds in a windowbox or flowerpot – keep sowing and keep picking.

4 large red peppers, preferably the long pointed kind (romano or ramira)

2 mozzarella cheeses, preferably *mozzarella di bufala*

4 handfuls of wild rocket

4 tablespoons best-quality, cold-pressed extra virgin olive oil

balsamic vinegar (optional)

sea salt and freshly ground black pepper

serves 4

tuscan panzanella

6 very ripe plum tomatoes

2 garlic cloves, sliced into slivers

4 thick slices day-old bread, preferably Italian-style, such as pugliese or ciabatta

about 10 cm cucumber, halved, deseeded and finely sliced diagonally

1 red onion, chopped

1 tablespoon chopped fresh flat leaf parsley

8–12 tablespoons extra virgin olive oil

2 tablespoons white wine vinegar, cider vinegar or sherry vinegar

a bunch of basil, leaves torn

12 caperberries or 4 tablespoons capers packed in brine, rinsed and drained

1 teaspoon balsamic vinegar (optional)

sea salt and freshly ground black pepper

serves 4

There are as many variations of this Tuscan bread salad as there are cooks – some old recipes don't even include tomatoes. The trick is to let the flavours blend well without allowing the bread to disintegrate into a mush. Always use the ripest, reddest, most flavourful tomatoes you can find – sweet Marmande, with its furrowed skin, is my favourite variety, or you could use one of the full-flavoured heirloom varieties, such as Black Russian or Green Zebra, or at least an Italian plum tomato.

Cut the tomatoes in half, spike with slivers of garlic and roast in a preheated oven at 180°C (350°F) Gas 4 for about 1 hour, or until wilted and some of the moisture has evaporated.

Meanwhile, put the bread on an oiled stove-top grill pan and cook until lightly toasted and barred with grill marks on both sides. Tear or cut the toast into pieces and put into a salad bowl. Sprinkle with a little water until damp.

Add the tomatoes, cucumber, onion, parsley, salt and pepper. Sprinkle with the olive oil and vinegar, toss well, then set aside for about 1 hour to develop the flavours.

Add the basil leaves and caperberries or capers and serve.

green vegetable salad
with hazelnut dressing

Green vegetables, like peas, beans, courgettes, asparagus and their kin, are favourites of mine. I mix them to serve as an accompaniment to hot dishes, but they are equally good as a cold salad. They live well together with the milder members of the onion family – pearl onions, baby spring onions or red onion. An ordinary vinaigrette will do as well, but I like nut oils such as macadamia, walnut and hazelnut, and they must be mixed with olive oil.

Microwave the asparagus tips, beans, courgettes, sugar snaps and green peas separately on HIGH for 2 minutes each, then transfer immediately to a bowl of ice cubes and water. This stops them cooking and sets the colour. Alternatively, bring a large saucepan of water to the boil, then add each vegetable and blanch until just tender, but still *al dente*. Keep the peas until the end, and drain well before chilling.

To make the dressing, put the olive oil, vinegar, mustard, salt and pepper in a salad bowl and beat well with a fork or small whisk to form an emulsion. Put in a bowl, add the drained vegetables, one kind at a time, and toss until lightly coated. Arrange the asparagus, beans, courgettes and spring onions on a serving platter or 4 rectangular salad plates. Add the sugar snaps and green peas, then sprinkle with hazelnut oil and toasted hazelnuts. Shave fresh Parmesan over the top and sprinkle with sea salt flakes and cracked black pepper.

notes

• Nut oils and nuts become rancid very quickly, so buy them in small quantities. Use them quickly, keep them sealed and store in the refrigerator, returning to room temperature for serving. Seed oils, such as pumpkin seed or sesame seeds, will suffer the same fate, so do the same with them.

• Green vegetables are one category of foods that perform well in the microwave, which is after all a kind of steaming.

about 12 mini asparagus tips

a handful of mini green beans (untrimmed)

4 mini courgettes, cut into thirds lengthways (optional)

100 g sugar snap peas

100 g shelled green peas

100 g mini spring onions

sea salt flakes and freshly cracked black pepper

fresh Parmesan cheese, to serve

hazelnut oil dressing

6 parts extra virgin olive oil

1 part Japanese rice vinegar or white wine vinegar

1/2 teaspoon Dijon mustard

hazelnut oil

75 g hazelnuts, pan-toasted in a dry frying pan, then lightly crushed into halves or big pieces

a little sea salt and freshly cracked black pepper

serves 4

carrot salad
with coriander curd

I always buy organically grown carrots, and try to find them with their leaves on. Although you can't eat carrot leaves, they are a good indication of how fresh the roots are. A wilted leaf is an old root. This recipe uses mustard oil, which may be new to you. It is available from Asian grocers, but if you can't find it, use another oil, but not olive. Mustard oil is related to oil made from oilseed rape, the plant that turns our countryside into a blanket of violently bright yellow. It is used in highly refined form to make oils such as vegetable oil or canola, although like most oils, it tastes better and is better for you when cold pressed – you do all the heating yourself in your own frying pan. Curd is another word for yoghurt.

375 ml plain yoghurt

3 medium carrots, with leaves, trimmed and peeled

2 tablespoons mustard oil or sunflower oil

1 tablespoon mustard seeds

1 medium green chilli, deseeded (optional) and finely sliced

2 tablespoons chopped coriander and a few sprigs of fresh coriander

2 sprigs of curry leaves (optional)

sea salt and freshly ground black pepper

serves 4

Put the yoghurt into a fine strainer and let drain over a bowl while you prepare the rest of the salad.

Using a mandoline or vegetable peeler, cut the peeled carrots into long ribbons. Bring a saucepan of lightly salted water to the boil, add the carrots, return to the boil and simmer for 2 minutes until limp but not soft. Drain, and rinse under cold running water.

Transfer to a serving bowl, curling the ribbons casually to leave space between them.

Put the oil in a small saucepan or frying pan, heat well, then add the mustard seeds, chilli and curry leaves, if using. Fry until the mustard seeds start to hop out of the pan (a little like popcorn), then pour the mixture over the carrots and let cool.

Put the yoghurt in a bowl and whip with electric beaters. Stir in the chopped coriander and spoon into a separate small bowl. Serve the 2 bowls together, topped with a few sprigs of coriander. To eat, take a share of the carrots and top with a spoonful of curds.

japanese cucumber salads

Japanese salads, like many Japanese dishes, are wonderfully elegant, often constructed as small towers in tiny bowls. They are usually simple affairs, with just a few elements, perfectly balanced. I love the Japanese way of preparing cucumbers – you sprinkle salt over a work surface, put the whole, unpeeled cucumber on top and roll it hard in the salt. Cut it in half lengthways, scrape out the seeds and slice it finely (a nifty little Japanese mandoline will do this perfectly for you). Rub the slices with salt, wash, drain and sprinkle with vinegar. It is a preparation method used in many cuisines and worth using in other dishes.

cucumber salad with ginger and seaweed

Prepare the cucumbers as described above, then put into a bowl, sprinkle with 1 teaspoon salt and rub lightly with your fingers. Wash, drain and sprinkle with a few drops of vinegar

Put the wakame in a bowl and cover with water. Cut out and discard any hard parts. Drain, then pour boiling water over the top, drain again and cut into 3 cm lengths. Put in a colander, sprinkle with a few drops of vinegar and set aside while you prepare the dressing.

Put the dressing, cucumber, wakame and prawns into a bowl and mix gently. Serve in small bowls with shreds of ginger on top.

crab and cucumber salad

Put the crab in a bowl, remove and discard any stray bits of shell, then sprinkle it with the vinegar and set aside.

Prepare the cucumbers as in the previous recipe – put salt on a cutting board and roll the cucumbers over the top. Cut in half lengthways, then slice thinly, using a mandoline, if you have one. Put into a strainer, sprinkle with salt and let drain for 30 minutes. Rinse with water, transfer to a dry cloth and squeeze out the liquid.

To serve, put a pile of cucumber in a tiny Japanese bowl, with a pile of crabmeat beside or on top, then sprinkle with the dressing and serve.

**cucumber salad
with ginger and seaweed**

2 mini cucumbers

1 teaspoon salt

rice vinegar (see method)

75 g wakame seaweed

1 recipe Sambai-zu Dressing
(page 26)

2–3 freshly cooked medium-to-large prawns, peeled and finely sliced crossways.

5 cm fresh ginger, peeled and sliced into fine shreds

crab salad

250 g white crabmeat

1/2 teaspoon rice vinegar

2 mini cucumbers

sea salt

1 recipe Kimi-zu Dressing
(page 26)

serves 4

nepali radish salad

The vegetable markets of Kathmandu are a riot of colour and, at least in the warm months, full of produce of extraordinary quality. The markets run at night too – I remember stumbling in the dark past shrines a thousand years old and women sitting beside lamps selling produce from their gardens. In Nepal, the radish is the white Asian kind, and it is usually blanched first. I added some red radishes to the dish to give some crunchy, peppery contrast.

Peel the mooli and cut into 5 cm pieces, then cut the pieces into chips about 1 cm square. Bring a saucepan of lightly salted water to the boil, add the mooli pieces and blanch for 3–4 minutes. Drain, dip into cold water, then drain and pat dry with kitchen paper. To prepare the red radishes slice them finely on a mandoline or cut into wedges.

Put the sesame seeds and mustard seeds into a dry frying pan and toast until they start to bounce. Stir in the turmeric, but do not let the seeds burn. Using a mortar and pestle, crush the spices together, then add the salt, pepper, lemon juice and oil and crush again. You can also use a small blender or spice grinder.

Put the mixture in a bowl, add the blanched mooli and toss gently until coated with the dressing. Add the red radishes and serve. This is good with other Indian dishes and rice.

notes

• I use a big stone mortar and pestle from Thailand to grind spices. Buy them from Asian markets, where they are relatively inexpensive. I also have a small coffee grinder that I use only for spices.

• This dressing is also good with other vegetables, such as new potatoes dressed with mint, chunks of blanched courgettes, or fresh soya beans (endomame) with chopped chilli and a handful of crushed peanuts.

• One of the best ways of serving radishes comes from France – trim them, provide small dishes of butter and sea salt and let your guests dip and crunch, a method that harks back to the original Roman idea of a salad.

½ mooli (daikon or Japanese white radish)

a bunch of red radishes, well washed

sea salt, to taste

sesame mustard dressing

4 tablespoons white sesame seeds

1 tablespoon mustard seeds

a pinch of turmeric

1 tablespoon freshly squeezed lemon juice

1 tablespoon mustard oil or peanut oil

sea salt and freshly ground black pepper, to taste

serves 4

indonesian gado gado

This is a terrific salad for a large party, and can be adapted for vegetarians if you leave out the shrimp. The original has all the ingredients lined up like soldiers, so you can take your pick of them. I think it's much nicer all higgledy-piggledy so the flavours have a chance to infuse. You can add and subtract ingredients according to what you have on hand and your own preferences.

To make the sauce, toast the peanuts in a dry frying pan, transfer to a tea towel and rub off the skins. When the nuts are cool, transfer to a blender and grind to a coarse meal. Add the chillies, onion, garlic, salt, sugar and coconut milk. Blend well, then transfer to a saucepan and cook until thickened. Set aside – the sauce will thicken further as it cools. When ready to serve, thin with water to the consistency of thin cream.

Bring a large saucepan of salted water to the boil and add the beans. Cook until *al dente*, about 1 minute, then remove to a sieve set over a bowl. Run cold water over them. When cool, transfer to a bowl of iced water. Just before serving, drain again and let dry in the colander.

Peel the pepper with a vegetable peeler. Cut off the top and bottom and remove the membranes, open out and slice thinly.

Put 2 tablespoons of the oil in a frying pan, dip the tofu in flour, then add to the frying pan and fry until brown on all sides. Drain and slice thickly.

To cook the shrimp crackers, fill a wok or saucepan two-thirds full of oil and heat until a piece of noodle will puff up immediately. Add the crackers, crowding them so they curl up. After about 3 seconds they should be puffed and airy. Remove and drain on kitchen paper.

Reheat the oil, add the onion rings and fry until crisp and golden. Remove and drain on kitchen paper.

Arrange all the ingredients on a large serving platter, drizzle with the peanut sauce, top with the onions and shrimp crackers, sprinkle with salt and serve.

a large handful of green beans, trimmed and halved

1 red or orange pepper

2 firm tofu cakes

flour, for dusting

½ packet shrimp crackers*

2 red onions, sliced

a large handful of beansprouts, rinsed, drained and trimmed

1 cos lettuce heart

15 cm daikon (mooli or white radish), peeled and cut into matchsticks

2 mini cucumbers, sliced, or 20 cm regular cucumber, halved lengthways and sliced

2 small hard-boiled eggs, quartered (cook so that the yolks are only just set, page 36)

sea salt

peanut oil, for cooking

peanut sauce

250 g shelled raw peanuts

2 red chillies, halved, deseeded and chopped

1 onion, finely chopped

1 garlic clove, crushed

1 teaspoon salt

2 teaspoons brown sugar

125 ml coconut milk

serves 4

*Shrimp crackers are sold in Asian shops in huge packets, but they last well. Keep the packet and serve shrimp crackers instead of crisps at your next party.

tomato salads

Tomato salads appear in infinite variety. My own favourite is a simple farmer's salad from my childhood. Good, ripe, sliced tomatoes, sprinkled with vinegar, salt and pepper. No oil. The salt brings out the tomato juices, which help form the dressing. We grew our own then, and the flavour was incomparable. I have put optional sugar in this first recipe to make up for the fact that, as everyone knows, tomatoes don't taste the way they used to! Heirloom varieties, like the Green Zebra shown, Black Russian or Brandywine, do have that old-fashioned flavour, so look out for them in farmers' markets.

tomato farmer's salad

Put the sliced tomatoes on a plate or in a bowl. Sprinkle with vinegar, salt and pepper and set aside for a few minutes until ready to serve. Taste, and add a pinch of sugar, if using.

tomato and onion salad

Cut 1 red onion in half lengthways, then slice it finely, separate the half-rings and put in the bowl. Slice the tomatoes and add to the bowl. Alternatively, use 6 spring onions, finely sliced diagonally. Proceed as in the previous recipe. Turn gently before serving.

tomato salad with dijon vinaigrette and herbs

Prepare the tomatoes as in the first recipe, then sprinkle with Dijon vinaigrette and turn them gently with 2 forks so as not to break up the tomatoes. Sprinkle with herbs, then serve.

moroccan-style tomatoes with preserved lemon and harissa vinaigrette (opposite)

To prepare the preserved lemons, cut them in quarters, scrape out and discard the flesh and cut the skin into strips. Put the vinaigrette, tomatoes, lemon strips and spring onions in a bowl. Mix gently, then toss in the mint. Set aside for a few minutes for the flavours to develop, then serve with mint leaves on top.

note

Preserved lemons are available in North African and French delicatessens. If unavailable, substitute the freshly grated zest of 2 unwaxed lemons.

4 large, ripe, flavourful tomatoes (1 per person), or 500 g mixed red and yellow cherry tomatoes, halved

tomato farmer's salad

3–4 tablespoons white wine vinegar

sea salt and freshly ground black pepper

sugar, to taste (optional)

tomato and onion salad

1 red onion or 6 spring onions

tomato salad with dijon vinaigrette and herbs

1 recipe Dijon Vinaigrette (pages 21, 83)

a handful of fresh herbs, such as torn basil leaves, scissor-snipped chives, or crushed thyme leaves

moroccan tomato salad with preserved lemon and harissa vinaigrette

1–2 preserved lemons

2 spring onions, chopped

1 recipe Harissa Vinaigrette (page 21)

1 tablespoon chopped fresh mint, plus a handful of leaves, to serve

serves 4

quick chickpea salad

Chickpeas are the basis of some of my favourite lunchtime salads and vegetable accompaniments for main courses. Like all dried pulses, they drink up flavours, but unlike some, chickpeas can be relied upon not to fall apart. They're great for picnics and other make-ahead occasions. You can part-prepare them, so the dressing soaks into the chickpeas, then add the fresh ingredients just before serving.

Put the dressing ingredients in a bowl and beat with a fork. Add the chickpeas, artichoke hearts and sun-blushed tomatoes, if using, and toss in the dressing. Cover and chill for up to 4 hours.

When ready to serve, add the cherry tomatoes, spring onions, basil, chives and parsley. Stir gently, then sprinkle with the shaved Parmesan and pepper.

note

Sun-blushed tomatoes, which are partly sun-dried tomatoes, are sold in Italian delis.

variations

• You can add any number of other ingredients, including olives, Parma ham, salami or chorizo, canned or char-grilled fresh tuna, other vegetables, leaves or herbs, or your favourite spices.

• Instead of Dijon dressing, dress with Basil Oil (page 30) or other herb oil. A few drops of chilli oil in the dressing instead of the mustard give a different kind of fire.

1 kg cooked or canned chickpeas, rinsed and drained

4 marinated artichoke hearts

4 large sun-blushed (semi-dried) tomatoes (optional)

250 g very ripe cherry tomatoes, halved

8 spring onions, sliced diagonally

a handful of basil, torn

a small bunch of chives, scissor-snipped

leaves from 4 sprigs of flat leaf parsley, chopped

50 g fresh Parmesan, shaved

1 tablespoon black pepper, cracked with a mortar and pestle

dijon dressing

6 tablespoons extra virgin olive oil

1 tablespoon freshly squeezed lemon juice or sherry vinegar

1 teaspoon Dijon mustard

1 small garlic clove, crushed

sea salt and freshly ground black pepper

serves 4

italian lentil salad

My favourite lentils are the tiny black French Puy lentils or the big Indian yellow channa dhaal. Other green or brown lentils are also good – though I draw the line at the red ones, toorvar dhaal. I think they turn into an unattractive pink mush. You don't need to soak lentils before cooking and, like beans, don't salt them until towards the end. You can also add aromatics such as onion, herbs, garlic or cinnamon stick to the cooking water. As a slothful cook however, one of my favourite late-night quick snacks is this salad using canned Italian lentils, which are a pretty maroon colour.

400 g cooked lentils, rinsed and drained

4 preserved baby artichokes, preferably char-grilled, quartered

1 red onion, halved lengthways and cut into fine slivered wedges

150 g feta cheese, cut into cubes or crumbled into big pieces

a handful of mixed fresh herbs, such as parsley, basil or marjoram, coarsely chopped, or chives snipped with scissors, to serve

italian dressing

a pinch of sea salt (taste the lentils first in case they're already salty)

1 tablespoon cider vinegar

3–4 tablespoons extra virgin olive oil

freshly ground black pepper

serves 4

Put the lentils in a bowl, then add the vinegar, oil and pepper.

Add the artichokes, onion and feta cheese, then toss gently. Add salt and pepper to taste, then serve, sprinkled with herbs.

variations

• Lentils with cherry tomatoes, black olives, chopped red onions and crushed garlic, dressed with a red wine vinegar vinaigrette. Add a few anchovy fillets (optional).

• Bocconcini or mozzarella cheese, torn into long shreds, with plum tomatoes, spring onions and basil. Add a sprinkle of balsamic vinegar before serving.

• Big ripe tomatoes, deseeded but with juices reserved, chopped into big pieces, mixed with preserved lemon peel or *mostarda di frutta* (from an Italian deli), with 1 tablespoon harissa paste added to the dressing.

• Shredded roasted chicken or crispy duck with wilted spinach and fried sage leaves.

note

Feta cheese is, of course, Greek or Cypriot, not Italian, but goes very well in this salad.

fish and
seafood

swedish crayfish party

August is crayfish season in Sweden, when the shops are full of special crayfish party paraphernalia – paper hats, paper lanterns with sunny faces, and candles for the table, even though the summer evenings are long and light. Freshwater crayfish are called crawdads in America and yabbies in Australia, but the dish is equally good made with large prawns. Serve with toast or crusty bread – plus good butter, glasses of icy aquavit (or vodka if you can't find it) and cold beer. Such a party is always for a big group, 6–8 people at least: serve 10–20 crayfish each, depending on size.

To cook the crayfish, start the day before. Put the salt, dill seed and bundle of dill into a large saucepan, add 2.5 litres water and bring to a rolling boil. Add the crayfish 5–6 at a time into the boiling water. Cover with a lid and simmer for about 5 minutes, or just until they turn red. Like all seafood, they shouldn't be cooked too long or they will be tough.

Remove the crayfish with a slotted spoon and transfer to a large bowl. Tuck more fresh dill between them. Put the saucepan into a sink of cold water to bring down the temperature quickly. When a little cooler, strain the liquid over the crayfish and let cool completely. Keep in the refrigerator overnight or up to 24 hours.

If using ready-cooked crayfish or prawns, put them into the bowl with fresh dill. Boil the water with salt, dill seed and bunch of dill, let cool, then strain over the crayfish and chill as before.

When ready to serve, drain the crayfish and pile generously onto a large serving platter. Top with the bunch of dill and serve with toast or bread, lots of good butter for spreading, aquavit or vodka and beer. Provide lobster crackers and picks, big napkins (I use white tea towels) and finger bowls.

To eat the crayfish, remove its claws and crack them. Eat the meat with your fingers. Pull off the tail and cut it down the side. Pull out the tail meat and remove and discard the dark thread. Eat on buttered toast or bread – or all alone. I like to serve them with a bowl of mayonnaise for dipping, but it's not traditional.

note

To serve iced aquavit, most Scandinavian households have a special decanter with dimpled sides. The liquor is decanted into the bottle and put into the freezer. Aquavit glasses are very elegant, like mini martini glasses.

10–20 uncooked crayfish or prawns per person

1 recipe Classic Mayonnaise (page 22), (optional)

dill marinade

2 tablespoons sea salt

3 tablespoons dill seed

a large bunch of fresh dill, tied up with string

to serve

a small bunch of fresh dill, preferably with flower heads

toast or crusty bread

unsalted butter

iced aquavit or vodka

beer

serves 4–6

greek octopus salad

This was one of my favourite summer salads when I lived in Sydney. The Sydney Fish Market, now a huge tourist attraction, used to be run by Greek fishermen, and Greeks are in love with octopus and squid. Octopus in Greece is banged against the ancient stone quay by handsome fellows straight out of *Shirley Valentine*. In Sydney, the octopus are put into a concrete mixer with a few shovels of ice and churned until tender. If you have a Greek fishmonger, he will remove the beak, eyes and insides. Otherwise – it's very easy.

1–2 octopus, cleaned (1–2 kg in total)

1 large potato, peeled but left whole

3 garlic cloves, crushed

a sprig of fresh oregano

2–3 sprigs of dill

green herb dressing (quantities depend on size of octopus!)

5–6 tablespoons extra virgin olive oil

freshly squeezed juice of 1/2–1 lemon

sea salt and freshly ground black pepper

a handful of basil, sliced

leaves from a sprig of oregano, chopped

1 tablespoon chopped fresh dill

to serve

sprigs of basil

sprigs of dill

2 tablespoons chopped fresh parsley

serves 8–10

Put the octopus in a large saucepan, bring to the boil, add the potato, garlic, oregano and dill and return to the boil. Reduce the heat and simmer until the potato is cooked. When it is cooked, so is the octopus: it will take about 30 minutes.

Remove the octopus from the pot (you can use the juice for a soup, but discard if making a salad). Cut the octopus into bite-sized pieces.

Put the dressing ingredients in a large bowl and beat with a fork. Add the octopus and toss to coat. Chill until ready to serve, topped with basil, dill and parsley.

notes

• To clean a large octopus, turn it upside down so the tentacles form a star. In the middle of the star is the hard beak. Cut it out and discard. Make a slit down the body of the beast and rinse out the guts. There is a quill inside (like a piece of transparent plastic) – remove it and give it to your budgie.

• If you don't want to cook the octopus whole, prepare it like a squid. Pull off the tentacles – the insides should come out too. Cut the tentacles off just above their join, so they make a star. Cut out the beak as before. Rinse out the body. Keep the tentacles and body and discard the rest.

mussels in ice wine

This way of cooking mussels is one of my favourite summer salads. It is based on the traditional recipe of mussels in white wine and garlic and I discovered it more or less by mistake. I was cooking a large quantity of mussels for a large lunch party, opening them in batches, then stopping them cooking by putting them on a bed of ice. Originally, I used a fruity, oaky Australian wine – but I have also tried this with mirin and sake (which is fabulous) and with grated ginger added and without the thyme or bay leaf. Note – don't add salt until you've tasted the dressing at the end. Mussel juice is very sea-salty and will probably have all the salt you need.

Put a layer of ice cubes into a small roasting dish and put a rack on top.

Put the wine, garlic, onion, thyme, bay leaf and parsley in a large saucepan and bring to the boil. Working in batches, add the prepared mussels, put on the lid and let steam until they open – just a minute or two each. Remove as they do so, take the empty shell off the top and put the mussel in its bottom shell on the rack over ice. Repeat until all have opened. When the mussels are cool, cover with clingfilm and keep in the refrigerator until ready to serve. Check from time to time that the melted ice isn't flooding them – pour it off if it does, so the water doesn't dilute the mussel flavour.

Strain the cooking liquid, let cool, then chill. It may be gritty, so strain through muslin if necessary. Put a serving platter in the freezer.

When ready to serve, spread a layer of ice cubes on the platter and arrange the mussels on top. Strew snipped chives over the mussels, then spoon the cooking liquid over the top. I think a sauce squeeze bottle would be useful for this – you need a little dressing in each shell.

note

To prepare mussels, rinse them under cold running water. Scrub off any mud with a small brush and discard any that seem heavy (they will be full of mud). If you like, you can scrape off any large barnacles, but they don't matter – they simply indicate that your mussels are free range. Pull off and discard any wiry beards. Tap each mussel against the work surface and discard any that don't close (that means it's dead). After cooking, discard any that haven't opened.

2 kg large mussels (see note)

250 ml fruity white wine, such as chardonnay

3 garlic cloves, crushed

1 small onion, chopped

a sprig of thyme

1 bay leaf

2 sprigs of parsley

a small bunch of chives, scissor-snipped

serves 4–6

spicy thai prawn salad

This salad is very simple – you can also make it with pre-cooked prawns. I cut them in half lengthways, so they're easier to eat, but also when stir-frying they curl into pretty corkscrews. When preparing the lemongrass and kaffir lime leaves, make sure to slice them very finely indeed. If you can't find them, use a squeeze of lemon juice and some grated regular lime zest instead. The grated zest of kaffir limes is much more scented and delicious than that of regular limes, which can be used if you can't find the real thing. *Kaffir* is a Hindi word meaning 'foreign', so throughout history people have thought these limes looked a little unusual.

1 tablespoon peanut oil

1 tablespoon red Thai curry paste

12 uncooked prawns, shelled, deveined and halved lengthways

12 cherry tomatoes, halved

a handful of mint sprigs, to serve

spicy thai dressing

1 stalk of lemongrass, outer leaves discarded, remainder very finely chopped

2 red bird's eye chillies, finely sliced and deseeded if preferred

2 pink Thai shallots or 1 small regular shallot, finely sliced lengthways

1 tablespoon brown sugar or palm sugar

freshly squeezed juice of 2 unwaxed limes

grated zest of 2 kaffir limes

a handful of fresh coriander leaves, finely chopped

3 spring onions, finely chopped

2 kaffir lime leaves, mid-rib removed, the leaves very finely sliced crossways, then finely chopped

serves 4

Heat the oil and curry paste in a wok, add the prawns and stir-fry for about 1 minute until opaque. Let cool.

To make the dressing, crush the lemongrass, 1 chilli and half the shallots with a mortar and pestle. Add the sugar, lime juice and zest and mix well until the sugar dissolves. Stir in the remaining chilli and shallots, and the coriander, spring onions and lime leaves.

Put the prawns into a serving bowl, add the cherry tomatoes, pour the dressing over the top and toss well. Serve, topped with mint.

variations

• This dressing is also good with crab claws – stir-fried or boiled.

• Use scallops instead of prawns. Prick the corals with a toothpick before cooking or they will explode in the heat.

• Try other Thai curry pastes, or a mixture of peanut oil and toasted sesame oil.

salade niçoise

Salade Niçoise is one of the classic composed salads. There has been much pontificating about the most authentic ingredients, but I think you can really use whatever you like from the basic list. Niçoise always seems to include tuna or canned anchovies or both; lettuce or tomatoes or both; eggs or potatoes or both; green beans or olives or both. They used to be arranged artfully in concentric circles on a large platter, but these days, more modern abstract forms in single servings seems to be the fashion. This makes a wonderful lunch for four or a starter for eight.

Cook the baby potatoes in boiling salted water until tender, about 10 minutes. Drain and plunge them into a bowl of iced water with ice cubes. Let cool. Drain, then toss in a little olive oil and cut in half.

Put the eggs in a saucepan of cold water, bring to the boil, reduce the heat and simmer for 5 minutes. Drain, then cover with cold water. When cool, peel, then cut in half just before serving.

Steam the broad beans and green beans separately until tender. Plunge into iced water, then pop each broad bean out of its grey skin. Alternatively, microwave the broad beans on HIGH for 3 minutes if fresh or 2 minutes if frozen, then refresh in iced water and peel as before. Microwave the green beans for 2 minutes, then plunge into iced water as before.

Blanch the spring onions for 30 seconds in boiling water. Drain and plunge into the iced water. Alternatively, leave uncooked, but trim and halve lengthways.

Finely slice the red onions and cucumbers, preferably on a mandoline – slice the cucumbers diagonally. If peeling the peppers, do so using a vegetable peeler, then cut off the top and bottom, open out, deseed and cut the flesh into thick strips.

Put the lettuce leaves on a platter. Add bundles of green beans and spring onions, then the potatoes, halved eggs, tomatoes, cucumber, onions and peppers. Top with anchovy fillets or tuna, black olives, caperberries or capers and basil leaves. Mix the vinaigrette ingredients in a small jug and serve separately.

note

You can tie up the bundles of the blanched green beans with blanched spring onion leaves.

10–12 small salad potatoes, such as Pink Fir Apples or Charlottes

4 small eggs

100 g shelled broad beans, fresh or frozen, or 6 cooked baby artichokes, halved

100 g green beans, stalks trimmed

3 spring onions, halved lengthways

2 small red onions, halved lengthways

2 mini cucumbers or 20 cm regular cucumber, unwaxed

2 red or yellow peppers, peeled (see method)

4 Little Gem baby lettuces or other soft lettuce leaves

1 punnet cherry tomatoes, about 20, halved

1 small can anchovy fillets, drained

1 large can or jar of good-quality tuna, drained

about 20 Niçoise black olives

about 20 caperberries or 3 tablespoons salt-packed capers, rinsed and drained

a large handful of fresh basil leaves

olive oil, for tossing the potatoes

vinaigrette

6 tablespoons extra virgin olive oil

1 tablespoon white wine vinegar, cider vinegar or sherry vinegar

1 teaspoon Dijon mustard (optional)

1 garlic clove, crushed

sea salt and freshly ground black pepper

**serves 8 as a starter,
4 as a main course**

tonno e fagioli

Tonno e fagioli – tuna and beans. I love this simple, delicious antipasti, discovered on my first trip to Italy, when every single thing I saw, heard and ate etched itself into my brain as the epitome of pleasure. Now I make it when I come home from work, all the shops have shut, and I've run out of almost everything. Though any dolphin-friendly canned tuna is fine, it will be fabulously good if you use top-quality French or Italian tuna, usually sold in jars, not cans – it will blow the budget of course, but why not! Cannellini beans can be delicate, so toss them gently. Though not traditional, I've also made this with chickpeas, lentils, borlotti beans and green flageolets, and sometimes use canned salmon instead of tuna. Easy, adaptable and good.

Put the garlic on a chopping board, crush with the flat of a knife, add a large pinch of salt, then mash to a paste with the tip of the knife. Transfer to a bowl, add the vinegar and 2 tablespoons of the oil and beat with a fork.

Add the beans and onions and toss gently. Taste, then add extra oil and vinegar to taste.

Drain the tuna and separate into large chunks. Add to the bowl and turn gently to coat with the dressing. Top with the basil and cracked black pepper.

note

For salads and dressings, I prefer young garlic. The older and drier it is, the more peppery it will become, so you will need less.

1–2 fat garlic cloves, crushed

1 tablespoon sherry vinegar or white wine vinegar

6 tablespoons extra virgin olive oil

600 g cooked or canned cannellini beans, rinsed and drained

2 red onions, finely sliced into petals, then blanched*, or 6 small spring onions, sliced

400 g best-quality tuna

a few handfuls of basil

sea salt and freshly ground black pepper

serves 6

Blanching is optional, but I think it takes the edge off the sharpness of the onions.

meat and poultry

french duck salade tiède

This is one of the classics of French cooking and a perfect example of what they call *salade tiède* or warm salad. It includes bitter leaves such as spinach, frisée and escarole, and the salad is topped with crisp bacon, in this case the French lardons, or batons of bacon. The cooking juices from the pine nuts, garlic and bacon are used to dress the salad. Without the duck, it can be served as a first course, or as an accompaniment to a main course. Many thanks to my friend, author and Michelin-starred chef Sonia Stevenson for teaching me this foolproof way of cooking duck breasts, which produces lots of wonderful duck fat for cooking sautéed potatoes later.

Put the duck breasts skin side down in a frying pan lightly brushed with olive oil. Sprinkle the flesh side with a little sea salt. Cook gently over low heat for 20–30 minutes to render out the fat – you will have to pour it off from time to time into a heatproof bowl. Take it slowly – the skin will gradually become crisp and golden and the fat line will almost disappear.

Turn the duck over and cook at high heat just to brown the flesh side – the interior should remain rare. Remove from the pan and let rest for about 5 minutes if serving hot, or 20 minutes if serving cool. Carve crosswise on a wooden board, making sure each slice has its share of crackling.

Put the spinach in a bowl, add the vinaigrette and toss lightly. Divide the leaves between 4 dinner plates or 8 starter plates.

Meanwhile, rinse and dry the frying pan. Reheat, add about 2 tablespoons olive oil, then the pine nuts. Toast over low heat, tossing gently, until golden on all sides, about 1 minute. Take care – they burn easily. Remove from the pan and let cool on a plate. Add the garlic to the pan and fry gently until crisp and golden brown. Remove to the same plate.

Add the bacon lardons and fry gently until crispy. Add the lardons to the salads, top with the pine nuts and garlic, then spoon the hot scented oil from the pan over the salads. Add freshly ground black pepper and serve.

variation

This is also good with pan-fried chicken livers.

4 duck breasts

500 g baby spinach leaves

4 tablespoons Vinaigrette (page 21), traditionally made with red wine vinegar

100 g pine nuts

3 garlic cloves, finely sliced

250 g bacon lardons, pancetta cubes or finely sliced smoked pancetta, as fatty as possible

sea salt and freshly ground black pepper

olive oil, for frying

serves 4 as a main course, 8 as a starter

vietnamese duck salad
with table salad herbs

You can use any cooked meat for this salad. In Chinatown, you can buy marvellous barbecued duck (and pork). The ducks are sold whole, halved or quartered. Just don't let the cook chop it up into chunks – it's better if you pull the duck off the bones in long shreds. Alternatively, butchers sell pairs of duck legs quite cheaply – everyone wants the breasts. So – if you rub them with a little salt and pepper, then roast them until the skin is crispy, they make a marvellous salad. You can use them to make a French or American-style salad, but I like this one, based on the traditional chicken and peanut salad, made of stir-fried chicken mince.

2 duck legs

4 handfuls of beansprouts, rinsed and drained

1 young carrot

6 spring onions, halved, then finely sliced lengthways

a handful of fresh mint leaves, preferably Vietnamese mint

a handful of Asian basil leaves (optional)

1 recipe Vietnamese Chilli-lime Dressing (page 25)

2 tablespoons pan-toasted peanuts, finely chopped

sea salt and freshly ground black pepper

serves 4

Rub the duck with salt and pepper and put into a preheated oven at 200°C (400°F) Gas 6 or higher. Roast until the skin is crisp and the meat tender, about 45 minutes–1 hour.

When cooked, remove and set aside until cool enough to handle. Pull the meat and crispy skin off the bones and discard the bones or keep them for stock. Try to use freshly cooked duck for salads, but if you must refrigerate it, reheat it before using. (Most meats, but especially fatty ones, are nicer if warm or cool, not cold.)

To trim the beansprouts, pinch off the tails and remove the bean from between the little leaves (optional).

To prepare the carrot, peel and shred into long matchsticks on a mandoline or the large blade of a box grater.

Pile the beansprouts on 4 plates. Add the carrot and duck and top with the spring onions, mint and basil leaves, if using. Sprinkle with the dressing, toss to coat with the dressing, top with the toasted peanuts, then serve.

variation

You may also add beanthread noodles to this salad. Soak 30 g noodles in hot water for 15 minutes, then drain and chop into short lengths with scissors. Keep the noodles in a bowl of cold water until ready to serve, then drain before adding to the salad.

insalata gonzaga

A marvellous, simple chicken salad named after the Gonzaga Dukes of Mantua, near Modena, the home of balsamic vinegar. True balsamic is rare and expensive, but use the best you can afford. This recipe comes from my Italian cousin, Tina Valentino-Capezza, who found this recipe in Milan.

Put the pine nuts in a dry frying pan and heat gently until lightly golden. Take care – they burn easily. Remove to a plate and let cool.

Put the chicken and radicchio in the bowl and toss gently. Sprinkle with sea salt, then with the vinegar. Toss gently with your hands. Sprinkle with olive oil and toss again. Taste, then add extra salt, vinegar or oil, as you wish.

Transfer to salad plates, sprinkle with the raisins, pine nuts, pepper and a few drops of balsamic vinegar and top with shards of Parmesan.

note

• For this salad, I soaked the raisins in verjuice for 10 minutes before adding to the salad. Verjuice is halfway between vinegar and wine, and can be found in delicatessens. Omit if unavailable.

• Note this Italian method of dressing salads – sprinkle first with salt, then with vinegar, toss, then sprinkle with oil. Taste, then add extra of any ingredient if necessary, to balance the flavours.

• If you prefer pepper leaves rather than bitter ones, this salad is also good with watercress instead of radicchio.

100 g pine nuts

250 g cooked boneless chicken, preferably breast, pulled into long shreds

1–2 heads of radicchio

1 tablespoon red wine vinegar, or to taste

6 tablespoons cold-pressed extra virgin olive oil, or to taste

4 tablespoons raisins, soaked in hot water for 10 minutes

1–2 tablespoons balsamic vinegar

sea salt and freshly cracked black pepper

100 g fresh Parmesan cheese at room temperature, cut into shards with a vegetable peeler

serves 4

warm chicken salad
with harissa dressing

Everyone loves a chicken salad – but it depends on the chicken. Roasted is gorgeous, poached is very good and char-grilled is best of all. The main thing, I think, is that the salad should be prepared while the chicken is still warm. Don't take a chilled chicken breast and chop it into bits. Not nice. Take the same breast, just after it's been cooked, and pull it into large pieces. It separates along the grain and tastes better and is more tender.

2 punnets ripe cherry tomatoes, or 4 sprays of cherry or plum tomatoes on the vine

½ garlic clove, crushed

olive oil, for roasting

4 freshly cooked chicken breasts

salad leaves

20 large green or black olives, pitted and halved

2 red onions, halved, then cut into thin wedges lengthways

sea salt and freshly ground black pepper

harissa dressing

6 tablespoons extra virgin olive oil

1 tablespoon harissa paste

1 tablespoon cider or sherry vinegar

serves 4

Put the tomatoes onto a baking sheet – if using vine tomatoes, put the whole vine on the sheet. Sprinkle with salt and olive oil, plus crushed garlic, and roast in a preheated oven at 200°C (400°F) Gas 6 or higher, until slightly charred and starting to collapse. Let cool, but do not chill.

Mix the dressing ingredients in a salad bowl and beat with a fork.

While still warm, pull the chicken into long chunks. Add to the bowl, then add the leaves, olives and onions and toss gently in the dressing.

Put onto salad plates, add the tomatoes and serve.

notes

• Pit and halve the olives yourself. Somehow, olives just taste better when you buy them with their pits in. Choose any kind – with garlic, chilli, lemon and herbs – whatever looks good on the day.

• I love dressings made with smoky, spicy harissa paste. Brands vary in heat, so add a little, taste, then add more if you prefer. Alternatively, you might like regular mustard instead.

turkey cobb salad

This American classic was invented in the Roaring Twenties by a Californian restaurateur named Cobb. It's essentially a 'bitser' salad – bitser this and bitser that – just like Niçoise or Gado Gado, two other legendary mixed salads. It's also a good post-turkey dish, when you have lots of turkey left over and you're looking for an effortless way to serve it. I always use the fattiest bacon or prosciutto – I can't see the point of bacon with no fat. Traditionally, the ingredients were arranged in lines. I've never liked that. Tumble it together. The dressing is not traditional, but I use it instead of mayonnaise – it is light and marvellous.

4 slices streaky bacon

2 Hass avocados

1 large butterhead lettuce

6 ripe plum tomatoes, cut into wedges

500 g cooked turkey, pulled into large shreds (page 17), at room temperature

2 hard-boiled eggs, quartered

100 g Roquefort cheese, cut into thin slices, or crumbled

olive oil, for cooking

lemon cream dressing

250 ml double cream

freshly squeezed juice of 1 lemon

a handful of chives, chopped

to serve

crusty rolls

mini cornichons, halved lengthways, or sliced gherkins

serves 4

Brush a frying pan with olive oil, add the bacon and cook until crispy but not crumbly. Remove and drain on crumpled kitchen paper.

Cut the avocados in half, remove the stones, then scoop out the flesh with a teaspoon.

Share the bacon, lettuce, tomatoes, turkey, eggs, cheese and avocado between 4 plates or bowls.

To make the dressing, put the cream in a bowl, add the lemon juice and beat well. Stir in the chives, then spoon over the salad and serve with crusty rolls and cornichons.

rare beef salad
with wasabi and watercress

A splendid special-occasion salad for a summer lunch party. When you serve it, cut the beef into thick slices, like steak. For the best flavour, let the meat return to room temperature first (it only takes a few minutes). Increase the amount of fillet to cater for the number of guests – since it's the same thickness, it will take the same time in the oven, no matter how big it is. Don't salt it first, or you'll draw out the juices. I like top-quality beef like this to be cooked absolutely plain, with any flavourings coming from the accompaniments. Wasabi is one of my favourite fiery condiments (I like it better than horseradish), because its spice is short, sharp and very strong.

Brush a heavy-based roasting tin with olive oil and heat on top of the stove until very hot. Add the beef and seal on all sides until nicely browned. Transfer to a preheated oven and roast at 200°C (400°F) Gas 6 for 20 minutes. Remove from the oven and set aside to fix the juices. Sprinkle with salt and pepper.

Let the meat cool to room temperature and reserve any cooking juices. If preparing in advance, wrap closely in foil and chill, but return it to room temperature before serving.

Arrange the leaves down the middle of a rectangular or oval serving dish. Slice the beef into 1 cm thick slices with a very sharp carving knife (or an electric knife). Arrange in overlapping slices on top of the leaves and pour any cooking juices from the roasting tin or carving board over the top.

Mix the mayonnaise with the wasabi paste and serve separately.

note

For a special-occasion dish like this, you simply must make the mayonnaise yourself. It's not difficult, especially if you have a food processor.

1 beef fillet, about 50 cm long, well trimmed

500 g watercress or other peppery leaves, such as wild rocket or, when in season, wild garlic (rampion)

sea salt and freshly ground black pepper

olive oil, for cooking

wasabi mayonnaise

1 recipe Classic Mayonnaise (page 22)

1 tube wasabi paste

serves 8

thai mango beef salad

The beef in this recipe is char-grilled but very rare. If you don't like rare meat, substitute something else, don't cook the meat until it's well done or even medium. I also like crispy roasted duck legs, poached chicken or prawns. The mango isn't traditional, but I like its juicy sweetness compared with the fiery chillies. Papaya is also good.

4 bundles of beanthread vermicelli noodles, about 30 g each (optional)

2 tablespoons dark soy sauce

1 tablespoon fish sauce

1 tablespoon brown sugar

500 g fillet of beef

4 small pink Thai shallots, or 2 regular, thinly sliced

1 Mini cucumber or 10 cm regular cucumber, thinly sliced

1 stalk of lemongrass, outer leaves removed and discarded, remainder very thinly sliced

dressing

4 tablespoons lime juice

4 tablespoons fish sauce

1 teaspoon brown sugar or palm sugar

to serve

1 ripe mango, peeled and cut into 1 cm cubes

2 red chillies, finely sliced diagonally

2 spring onions, thinly sliced

a large handful of mint leaves

serves 4

If serving with noodles, put them in a bowl and cover with hot water. Let soak for about 15 minutes, then drain. Keep in a bowl of cold water until ready to serve, then drain and cut into short lengths, about 5–10 cm, with kitchen scissors.

Put the soy, fish sauce and sugar into a bowl and beat with a fork to dissolve the sugar. Add the beef and turn to coat. Set aside for 1–2 hours to develop the flavours. When ready to cook, preheat a barbecue or stove-top grill pan until very hot. Put the meat on the barbecue or pan and cook slowly, turning from time to time, until the surface is well browned and the middle still pink, about 5 minutes in total, depending on the thickness of the meat. Remove from the heat and set aside in a warm place for about 5 minutes to set the juices.

Put the meat on a board and slice thinly crossways. Cut the slices into bite-sized strips about 5 cm long.

Mix the dressing ingredients in a large bowl, beating with a fork to dissolve the sugar. Add the beef slices and any meat juices, the shallots, cucumber and lemongrass. Toss well.

Put a pile of noodles, if using, onto each plate, then add the dressed salad. Add the mango, chillies and spring onions, then spoon any remaining dressing from the bowl over each serving. Top with mint leaves and serve.

note

I prefer mini or 'Lebanese' cucumbers, which aren't as watery as the regular kind. If you can't get them, use part of an ordinary one, but cut it in half lengthways and scrape out the seed section before slicing. I always look for unwaxed cucumbers – if they're waxed, you'll have to peel them, which rather defeats the purpose. You can also cut 4 lengthways strips out of the skin with a canelle knife if you yearn for more decoration.

pasta, rice and
noodles

couscous salad
with mint and coriander

I have yet to meet a pasta salad I could love – other than couscous. This very quick and easy salad is endlessly adaptable. Omit the chicken and add other uncooked or lightly blanched vegetables, such as cucumber, baby carrots, cherry tomatoes, sugar snap peas, asparagus tips or herbs. Easy-cook couscous is supposed to be just soaked then drained, but I find it's better for a little more microwaving or steaming after soaking. It should be dry and fluffy.

4 tablespoons couscous

125 ml boiling chicken stock or water

6 sun-blushed (semi-dried) tomatoes or 6 fresh cherry tomatoes, halved

2 marinated artichoke hearts, sliced

3–4 spring onions, sliced

400 g canned chickpeas, rinsed and drained

harissa dressing

6 tablespoons extra virgin olive oil

1 tablespoon sherry vinegar or cider vinegar

1 tablespoon harissa paste

sea salt and freshly ground black pepper

to serve

a handful of flat leaf parsley, coarsely chopped

sprigs of watercress

sprigs of mint

sprigs of coriander

snipped chives

serves 2

Put the couscous in a heatproof bowl and cover with the stock or water. Leave for 15 minutes until the water has been absorbed. For a fluffier texture, put the soaked couscous in a strainer and steam over simmering water for another 10 minutes, or microwave in the jug or bowl on 50 per cent for about 5 minutes. Drain if necessary, pressing the liquid through the strainer with a spoon, then fluff up with a fork. Let cool.

When ready to make up the salad, put the couscous in a bowl, add the tomatoes, artichoke hearts, spring onions and chickpeas. Keep the watercress and herbs in a separate container until just before serving.

To make the dressing, put the olive oil, vinegar and harissa paste in a bowl and beat with a fork. Add salt and pepper to taste. Sprinkle half the dressing over the couscous mixture and toss with a fork. Add the watercress and herbs and serve. Serve the extra dressing separately for people to help themselves.

variation

This is a perfect picnic, lunchbox or make-ahead salad. Put the watercress and herbs into a small container and seal. Put the dressing ingredients in a screw-top jar, and shake to mix. Shake again just before serving. Put the couscous and remaining ingredients in a lidded plastic bowl, and seal until ready to use. To serve, add the dressing, parsley and watercress and toss well.

japanese soba noodle
salad with prawns

One of the great Japanese cold dishes, in which the quality and flavour of the buckwheat can be especially savoured. Soba noodles are an elegant fawn colour, and there is a beautiful green-tea-flavoured, pale green version know as cha-soba (*cha* means 'tea' in many languages). Other noodles, such as somen or thick udon noodles, are also good this way.

400 g dried soba noodles, brown or green

12 dried shiitake mushrooms

2 tablespoons Japanese soy sauce (tamari)

2 tablespoons mirin (Japanese sweetened rice wine) or dry sherry

12 uncooked prawns

12 spring onions, finely sliced

4 teaspoons furokaki pepper (optional)

4 teaspoons wasabi paste

ice cubes

dipping sauce

250 ml dashi stock*

2 tablespoons mirin (Japanese sweetened rice wine) or dry sherry

a pinch of sugar

3 tablespoons Japanese soy sauce (tamari)

serves 4

*Dashi is available in powder or concentrate form in Japanese shops and some supermarkets. Dissolve 1 teaspoon in 250 ml hot (not boiling) water, or to taste.

Put the dipping sauce ingredients in a saucepan, simmer for about 5 minutes, then chill.

Cook the noodles for 5–6 minutes or according to the packet instructions. Drain, rinse in cold water and cool over ice. Chill.

Put the shiitakes in a saucepan, cover with 250 ml boiling water and soak until soft. Remove and discard the mushroom stems. Add the mushrooms to the pan.

Add the soy sauce and mirin to the pan, bring to the boil and simmer for a few minutes to meld the flavours. Add the prawns and simmer for about 1 minute until firm. Drain, reserving the cooking liquid. Shell the prawns, but leave the tail fins intact. Devein and split each prawn down the back to the fin, giving a butterfly shape. Chill the prawns and poaching liquid. Just before serving, dunk the chilled noodles in the liquid, then drain.

To serve, half-fill a lacquer bowl with ice and water, then add the noodles. Serve the prawns, spring onions and mushrooms separately. Let your guests assemble their salads themselves. Serve with separate dishes of furokaki pepper, if using, wasabi paste and dipping sauce.

japanese tofu salad
with sesame seeds

If you're not a tofu fan, this elegant, simple recipe is where to start your love affair. It is made with silken tofu, a name that describes its texture. It should be eaten very fresh, and if you bring it home in a carton with water, drain off the water and cover with fresh cold water. It will keep for several days if you change the water daily. The tofu won't fall apart so easily if you firm it up by pressing between two plates – a method I saw demonstrated by Japanese food writer Kimiko Barber at Books for Cooks in London's Notting Hill.

2 blocks silken tofu, well chilled

dipping sauce

4 tablespoons soy sauce
(I prefer to use wheat-free tamari)

1 tablespoon sugar

4 tablespoons sake

250 ml dashi*

to serve

2 tablespoons white sesame seeds

2 spring onions, finely sliced

5 cm fresh ginger, peeled and finely grated

serves 6

Dashi is available in powder or concentrate form in Japanese shops and some supermarkets. Dissolve 1 teaspoon in 250 ml hot (not boiling) water, or to taste.

Put the dipping sauce ingredients into a small saucepan and heat slowly until the sugar has dissolved. Cool and chill.

Put the tofu blocks carefully on a flat plate and invert another plate over them. Put a weight, like a can of beans, on top and set aside for at least 30 minutes. Set it on a tilt on the draining board (put a chopstick under the plate) to drain out some of the moisture. Keep cold.

Put the sesame seeds in a dry frying pan and toast gently until aromatic. Do not let burn.

To serve, take a block of tofu in one hand and carefully cut in 3 both ways – you will end up with 9 cubes. Repeat with the second block of tofu. Either put all the tofu into a glass serving dish, or put 3 in each person's bowl. Serve a bowl of sesame seeds, spring onion and grated ginger, and another bowl with the dipping sauce to each person.

black rice salad
with chilli greens

I have a passion for Asian rice, with its subtle flavours and special uses. I've tried various kinds in salads and, apart from very sticky rice, most are great. My favourite is Asian black rice – if you can't find it, use wild rice. The main thing is that you should never put rice in the refrigerator. Boil it, cool it, make the salad and serve it as fast as possible. And if you're not going to serve it straight away, put sushi vinegar through it as it's cooling, in order to flavour and preserve it. The result is utterly wonderful.

Put the dressing ingredients into a saucepan, bring to the boil and simmer until the sugar has dissolved. Taste and add water if necessary. Cool.

To make the sushi vinegar, put the vinegar, sugar, salt, ginger and garlic into a saucepan and simmer over low heat.

Put the rice into a saucepan, cover with water to 1 finger's joint above the top of the rice and bring to the boil. Cover tightly with a lid, reduce the heat and simmer for 14 minutes (12 for white rice). Turn off the heat, do NOT remove the lid, and set aside for 12 minutes. Remove the lid. The rice should be perfectly fluffy. If not (and this sometimes happens with black rice), put the lid back on and boil hard for about 1 minute. Remove from the heat, drain, then run it under cold water. Drain again.

Transfer to a bowl, sprinkle with the sushi vinegar and stir it through gently with a spoon.

Put the asparagus stalk ends into a saucepan of boiling salted water for 1½ minutes or until you can just pierce them with a fork. Scoop out and drain in a colander under cold running water. Add the tips and sugar snaps and cook as before for about 30 seconds, until just tender. Drain under cold running water. Cook the green beans and broad beans, if using, in the same way.

Put all the greens in a bowl, add the chilli and spring onions and mix well.

Add the chilli greens to the rice and sprinkle with the dressing. Stir gently, then serve.

note

This recipe is Asian. However, you can alter its emphasis by changing the dressing to a regular Vinaigrette (page 21) and, for instance, using red onion instead of spring onion, and omitting the chilli.

250 g Asian black rice or your choice of other rice

asian dressing

2 stalks of lemongrass, outer leaves discarded, remainder very finely chopped

3 cm fresh ginger, peeled, grated and juice squeezed

1 green chilli, halved, deseeded and finely chopped

freshly squeezed juice of 1 lime

125 ml fish sauce

2 tablespoons brown sugar

sushi vinegar

140 ml Japanese rice vinegar

5 tablespoons sugar

4 teaspoons salt

5 cm fresh ginger, peeled, grated and squeezed

3 garlic cloves, crushed

chilli greens

a handful of asparagus, halved

a handful of sugar snap peas

a handful of green beans, halved

100 g broad beans, boiled and skinned (optional)

1 chilli, deseeded and chopped

4 spring onions, sliced diagonally

serves 4

websites and mail order

salad plants and seeds

Suffolk Herbs
Tel: 01376 572456
www.suffolkherbs.com
Salad vegetables and organic seeds.

Halcyon Seeds
10 Hampden Close, Chalgrove,
Oxfordshire OX44 7SB
Tel: 01865 890180
www.halcyonseeds.co.uk
Seeds for herbs, vegetables and salad
leaves. Online ordering/catalogue.

**Marshalls Vegetable Seed
Company**
S.E. Marshalls & Co Ltd,
Freepost PE787, Wisbech,
Cambs PE13 2WE
Tel: 01945 466711
www.marshalls-seeds.co.uk
All you need for a kitchen garden.

The Organic Gardening Catalogue
Riverdene, Molesey Road,
Hersham, Surrey KT12 4RG
Tel: 01932 253666
www.organiccatalog.com
Organic seeds including herbs, salads.

Simpson's Seeds
The Walled Garden Nursery,
Frome Road, Horninghsham,
Somerset BA12 7NQ
Tel: 01985 845004
www.simpsonsseeds.co.uk
Salad vegetables including chillies.

food suppliers

Selfridges Food Hall
Selfridges, 400 Oxford Street,
London W1A 1AB
Tel: 020 7318 3899

Graig Farm Organics
Tel: 01597 851655
www.graigfarm.co.uk
Organic fish, dairy produce, groceries,
fruit, vegetables and organic alcohol.

Organics Direct
Tel: 01604 791911
www.organicsdirect.co.uk
Home delivery of organic food boxes.

West Country Organics
West Country Organics Ltd,
Natson Farm, Tedburn St Mary,
Exeter, Devon EX6 6ET
Tel: 01647 24724
www.westcountryorganics.co.uk
Delivers food boxes weekly nationwide,
including salads and herbs.

HERBS, SPICES AND OILS
Cool Chile Company
PO Box 5702, London W11 2GS
Tel: 0870 902 1145
www.coolchile.co.uk
Dried chillies and Mexican ingredients.

**Extra Virgin Olive Oils and
Mediterranean Foods**
Tel: 01460 72931
www.getoily.com
Olive oils and Mediterranean produce.

Fox's Spices
Fox's Spices, Dept GF,
Masons Rd, Stratford upon Avon,
CV37 9NF
Tel: 01789 266 420
Mail order catalogue for herbs, spices.

Peppers by Post
Sea Spring Farm, West Bexington,
Dorchester, Dorset DT2 9DD
Tel: 01308 897766
www.peppersbypost.biz
Mail order for fresh, home-grown
chillies in season (July–December).

The Spice Shop
Tel: 020 7221 4448
www.thespiceshop.co.uk
Fresh spices, blends and herbs.

FISH
The Fish Society
Tel: 0800 074 6859
www.thefishsociety.co.uk
Fresh fish including organic and wild
salmon, smoked fish and shellfish.
Next day delivery.

Seafooddirect
Tel: 0800 851549
www.seafooddirect.co.uk
Home delivery of fish and seafood.

Wing of St Mawes
Tel: 0800 052 3717
www.wingofstmawes.co.uk
Fresh and smoked fish. Next
day delivery.

POULTRY AND MEAT
The Country Butcher
Tel: 01452 831585
www.countrybutcher.co.uk
Award-winning sausages and
traditional bacon.

Providence Farm Organic Meats
Tel: 01409 254421
www.providencefarm.co.uk
Organic pork, beef, chicken and duck.

Scottish Organic Meats
Tel: 01899 221747
www.scottishorganicmeats.com
Organic beef, lamb and pork.

ASIAN FOOD SUPPLIERS
Sri Thai (Thai)
56 Shepherd's Bush Road, London
W6 7PH
Tel: 020 7602 0621

Super Bahar (Iranian and Middle
Eastern)
349 Kensington High Street,
London W8 6NW
Tel: 020 7603 5083

Talad Thai (Thai, South-east Asian)
320 Upper Richmond Road,
London SW15 6TL
www.taladthai.co.uk
Tel: 020 8789 8084

Tawana Oriental Supermarket (Thai)
18 Chepstow Road, London W2 5BD
Tel: 020 7221 6316

Thanh Xuân Supermarket
(Vietnamese)
84 Deptford High Street,
London SE8 4RG
Tel: 020 8691 8106

TK Trading (Japanese)
Unit 7, The Chase Centre, Chase
Road, North Acton, London
NW10 6QD
Tel: 020 8453 1743
www.japan-foods.co.uk (in Japanese)

ASIAN SPECIALIST FOOD DISTRICTS
Southall, Tooting and Wembley
Three areas full of Indian, Bangladeshi
and Pakistani grocers and shops,
stocking a wide range of South Asian
spices and ingredients.

Edgware Road, London
Lebanese and Middle Eastern spices
and ingredients.

Gerrard Street area, Soho, London
Chinese, Japanese, South-east Asian.

index